T0131785

SHORTS
THAT
FIT WELL

A COLLECTION OF INSPIRATIONAL SHORT STORIES

WAYNE E. BEYEA

iUniverse®

SHORTS THAT FIT WELL
A COLLECTION OF INSPIRATIONAL SHORT STORIES

iUniverse books may be ordered through booksellers or by contacting:

iUniverse
1663 Liberty Drive
Bloomington, IN 47403
www.iuniverse.com
1-800-Authors (1-800-288-4677)

ISBN: 978-1-5320-8559-8 (sc)
ISBN: 978-1-5320-8413-3 (hc)
ISBN: 978-1-5320-8414-0 (e)

Library of Congress Control Number: 2019916143

Print information available on the last page.

iUniverse rev. date: 11/08/2019

CONTENTS

SHORTS THAT FIT WELL

INTRODUCTION
OF AUTHOR

Wayne E. Beyea, is a versatile author. He has penned fiction novels, his autobiography, a biography, a true crime story and is now introducing a compilation of short stories that are certain to inspire positive emotions in all readers.

While ensconced in his second career, Author Beyea, commenced writing a monthly article for the glossy North Country business magazine "Strictly Business."

After hearing a news bulletin concerning our nation's President, Beyea was inspired to pen his first book, "Fatal Impeachment," a crime fiction novel with an intriguing plot and a surprise ending."

"Reflections From the Shield", consisting of over 1000 pages, and produced in two books followed. RFTS is an autobiography depicting the author's exciting career as a member of the New York State Police.

The author next produced "The Day the Catskills Cried", a true-crime story detailing the kidnapping and murder of New York socialite Trudy Resnick Farber.

"The "Captain of the Juniper", the life story of Lake Champlain cruise ship Captain Frank Pabst followed. Captain Pabst was well known in the Lake Champlain region. The Captain led a very interesting life and is somewhat of a legend in the North Country of New York.

A return to fiction resulted in the novel, "The Treasure of Valcour Island", an exciting tale of greed and murder related to the discovery of sunken treasure.

"The Twentieth Terrorist" a tale of excitement and intrigue connected to the terrorist plot on 9/11/01 followed and is the sequel to "The Treasure of Valcour Island.

Readers are now treated to "Shorts That Fit Well" a collection of both fiction and true short stories intended to inspire smiles and positive emotions. Read, relax, enjoy and smile!

SHORTS THAT FIT WELL

SAMANTHA

Our children were first to spot the pile of dirty, bloody fur, lying at our back door. Patrick, Mary, Nannette and Eric, ages 10 – 9 – 8 and 6 respectively, announced in unison: "Mommy, Daddy, a puppy! Can we keep him?" The pile of burr filled fur at our door was hardly a puppy. It was the sorriest looking excuse for a dog I had ever seen. I gazed upon a mutt about one-year old. Blood oozed from a wound in the animal's side. I thought, '*it's probably the injury, hunger and exhaustion that brought this animal to our door.*' Despite its miserable appearance, the dog had friendly, dark brown eyes that emitted a, 'please help me look.' It wore no collar or license and I considered calling the SPCA to have the poor thing disposed of, but, a warm elegance shone in those dark eyes and that look convinced me this mysterious animal deserved a better fate. I told our pleading children that the dog could stay with us until we found its owner. They squealed with joy and set about finding something for the dog to eat. They carefully served up a dish of cat food and bowl of milk which the animal quickly devoured, licking both dishes sparkling clean.

Our children hovered over the dog while it ate and after it had consumed the feline meal, they decided it was time to introduce the dog to Kitty. Kitty had entered our house as a wee kitten and after being pampered and spoiled for five-years, was not about to welcome an interloper into her domain! Especially when the interloper was a Dog! Kitty stared contemptuously at the dog from a distance with static fur, emitting a growling hiss, intended to let the disgusting animal know it was not welcome in her house. The dog wisely respecting Kitty's claws, kept its distance and tried to gain acceptance by whining and wagging its tail.

My wife (a Registered Nurse), treated the dog's wound, brushed the burrs out of its fur and gave it a bath. The dog was submissive, even cooperative, and when clean, the long haired, medium size dog was quite beautiful. Its coat was entirely black and white except for a small patch of brown over each eye. This characteristic gave the dog a Collie facial appearance.

We didn't locate the dog's owner and I must confess, I didn't try very hard.

The dog's heritage would remain a mystery, but it was obvious that this animal had come from an environment that included children. The dog loved children and it poured out its love to our children. Yes, it was just a mutt, but to our kids this dog was the purest of pure breeds, delivered to them by divine providence. Although the dominant breed of the dog was a mystery, its gender was no mystery, it was a female.

I explained to our children that the dog was about one-year old, most likely had a name and would probably respond to its name. Mary started the name search. She stared intently into the dog's face and said, "Sam is your name Sam?" The dog responded by wagging its tail and yipping excitedly. Our kids screamed excitedly, "That's it! Our dog's name is Sam." They had seen sufficient proof that Sam was the dog's name. I tried to explain that as the dog was a female, it was unlikely its name was Sam. However, they were convinced and I could not argue with the logic offered by Patrick, "Dad, Sam is her nickname. Her full name is Samantha, and she answers to Sam." So it was that Sam or Samantha, depending on who was calling her, became the eighth member of our family.

Samantha soon proved that she possessed superb intelligence and good manners. Her excellent behavior and affection for children led us to believe she had come from a disciplined environment that included children. It was evident she had been disciplined because when we spoke to her in a gruff tone of voice, she put her head between her legs and assumed a cowering position.

Whether motivated by respect or fear, Sam maintained a safe distance from Kitty. However, she had a gourmet taste for cat food and hovered about Kitty while she ate, hoping that Kitty would leave some food for her. Kitty often responded with arched back, static fur and warning growl. At these times, Sam always chose discretion over valor and backed off while wagging her tail to indicate she was only being friendly. When Kitty had finished eating and strutted from the room, Sam hurried to Kitty's dish and licked it clean.

Samantha had been with us only a few weeks when it became obvious that chastity was not one of her virtues. Her stomach and breasts were swelling and it was obvious that the swelling was not from her ingestion of cat food, but the result of an assignation. Our veterinary confirmed this suspicion, informing us that Samantha was soon to become a mother. Although I had grown fond of Sam and welcomed her adoption into our family, I had misgivings about turning our home into a kennel. Our house was too small for more than one dog, and for awhile, I considered having Sam aborted and spayed. However, our kids knew Sam was expecting and they eagerly looked forward to being able to cuddle puppies. How could I deprive them the wonderful experience of seeing newborn puppies? I explained to our children that Sam would be allowed to deliver her puppies and then we would find homes for them.

Sam had been living the good life just being our family dog, but as an expectant mother, she languished in luxury. She was pampered and spoiled by two concerned adults and four young mid wives. When the blessed day arrived, Sam disappeared. We called and searched for her to no avail and six worried minds envisioned the worst. She had been dog-napped! She was hopelessly lost in the woods! She was caught in a trap! Someone had shot her! She had been hit by a car! Our anxiety increased and panic was defeating rational thought. Strained, worried faces, suddenly developed smiles when Eric shouted that he could see Sam lying under our tool shed. We coaxed and pleaded with her to come out, but our pleas fell on deaf ears. She ignored enticements of dog food, milk, dog biscuits, and even her favorite, cat food. She pretended to be oblivious of our presence. Finally, little Eric wriggled under the shed and pushed Sam out of her adopted birthing den. I carried her into the house and placed her in a large box lined with old blankets that was designed by my wife as an appropriate birthing room. Although not the maternity suite of her choice, Sam settled in and did her best to ignore four little kids who worried over her like expectant fathers. Awestruck over the uncertainty of how birth occurs and what they would see and not wanting to upset Sam, they sat staring into the box and conversed in whispers. They watched and waited until late evening. Finally, exhaustion took its toll and one by one, they succumbed to sleep. Mother and Dad outlasted kids, but finally, we gave up and went to bed.

Suddenly, my sleep was shattered by screams! I sat up in bed trying to comprehend what was happening and came to the realization that the screams I heard were screams of excitement and joy. "Mommy, Daddy! Come quick, our children shouted, "Puppies!" I got out of bed, fumbled with my bathrobe and while so engaged, the adage, "A watched pot never boils," came to mind. Kathy and I joined our excited children in the delivery room and joyously shared the glory of the moment. Six mouse sized puppies squeaked and groped searching for milk spigots. Sam, lying on her side, looked exhausted, but her face had a contented look and seemed to ask, "Well, how do you like my babies?" Our kids oohed and ahhed over the puppies and gently stroked Sam's head. The pups certainly were cute, but evidenced genetic fallout. There were two Beagles, two Shepherds and two Poodles; or, two Collies, two Saint Bernard and two hounds; or perhaps two…? In essence, they were mutts. The dominant breed of each was left to the eye of the beholder. I had to admit that despite their lack of established heritage, these pups were beautiful and as I watched my wife and children happily cuddling these unique creatures, I silently gave thanks to God for sending Sam into our lives.

Sam handled motherhood in a most professional manner. She kept her babies clean and generally tolerated the abuse six playful, hungry pups, subjected her to. Occasionally however, an overzealous pup would attempt to get milk from a part of her anatomy that didn't provide it, or, bite the part that did, resulting in a nipping reprimand. The offender's yips would usually bring a child to cuddle it and kiss away the pain.

Kitty treated the puppy invasion with disdain and polite indifference. She would pay an occasional visit to the canine nursery, peer intently over the edge of the box, then stroll away with a disgusted look on her face. I wondered what she was thinking and envisioned her thoughts as, "Perhaps if I ignore the ugly things they will leave me alone and go away." Six inquisitive, playful puppies were certainly not about to ignore a cat. As soon as they were able to fall out of the nursery box, Kitty became an object of curiosity and their quarry. They stalked her around the house and when fortunate enough to find her sleeping pounced on her tail, or jumped around her yapping excitedly. They wallowed in her food dish and annoyed her while she ate by feigning an attack. Kitty was surprisingly tolerant and usually suffered the abuse in silence. Infrequently, she let a pesky pup know she had taken enough with a slap in the nose. That would send the puppy yipping for the sympathy of a kid or protection of its mother.

As the four male and two female puppies grew, they started to develop individual personalities and looks. The largest, a male, was roly-poly, slow witted, had dark fuzzy hair, a poodle face and was always content. Our children named him Gus. The next largest puppy – also a male – looked a lot like Gus, but had wiry, white hair and a perpetual smile, which earned him the name Smiley. The children named the third largest; a whiney male with Beagle markings but a scrunched up bulldog face, Chopper. The remaining male had Beagle markings, a sad hound looking face and was gangly on his feet. This clumsy little pup, the epitome of a mutt, earned the name, Muttley. Both female puppies had prominent brown and white beagle markings and both were petite. One had four white paws, which earned her the name Boots. Boots was a beautiful animal but she was headstrong and aloof. She disliked being held and would struggle to get away from whomever tried to hold her. She would tolerate being petted but did not enjoy it and never solicited it. Boot's sister was just the opposite. She had a sweet, loving disposition and pigged out on affection. Our children thought she was a Princess and that is what they named her.

Sam and her children provided our children with countless hours of pleasure. As the days passed, the puppies grew larger, more curious and their play became rougher. They pestered Kitty unmercifully and frequently tried Sam's patience with their antics. Our little home was becoming a kennel and we knew it was time to put the pups out for adoption. My wife psyched our kids on the importance of finding a good home for each puppy. They set about convincing friends just how much they needed a puppy and once the prospect had cuddled a puppy, it was difficult for their parents to say no. Clumsy, adorable Gus, was first to go, followed by Smiley, Princess and Chopper. Homely Muttley and beautiful but unsociable Boots, were passed over and remained with us.

Sam started teaching Muttley and Boots how to hunt as soon as they were able to run. She would lead the pups into woods behind our house and they would be gone for hours. Occasionally, we could hear Muttley's squeaky imitation of a hound baying and Boots puppy yips, indicating they were hot on the trail of something. We did not worry about the pups while they were in the woods because we trusted that Sam would take care of them and they enjoyed their freedom. Of course their wandering could bring them into the clutches of a dog warden, but Sam was now prepared for this eventuality with a license. Sam wore her license on a fine leather collar which she did not appreciate. The puppies had inherited natural hunting instincts, loved to roam the woods and we could not deny them this pleasure. The elusive rabbit was their favorite quarry, but to my knowledge, they never caught one.

As both puppies grew, Sam – probably because of a personality clash with Boots – became more attached to Muttley and detached from Boots. Muttley had inherited his mother's warm, friendly, loving disposition and would constantly seek affection from every member of our family. Beautiful Boots, remained independent, aloof, would not show affection and hated being held. Boots unfriendly behavior was a mystery, but it was no mystery that she loved to hunt and that was what she was doing when she disappeared. We never learned her fate, but, I prefer to believe she was picked up by someone who would love and care for her. That explanation seemed to ease our children's anxiety and besides, Boots had not been as endearing as Muttley.

Sam seemed unconcerned about Boots disappearance and continued her daily foray into the woods accompanied by Muttley. Sam often returned home alone, but there was no need to worry about Muttley. He simply tracked his mother's scent and arrived home sometime later. In fact, I believe Sam intentionally abandoned him in the woods, just to test his tracking ability. Muttley's first love became hunting and he would rather be chasing a rabbit than eating. One day, Muttley, just shy of six months old, was hot on the puffy tail of a bunny that hopped across a road. The bunny made it safely across, but Muttley did not. Muttley's death was very traumatic and especially so for our children. They grieved deeply and it was difficult to provide any words that would ease their pain. Wiping away our own tears, Kathy and I offered that Muttley's spirit was happily chasing bunnies in doggie heaven and although we would miss him, he had just gone to a better place. This helped to slightly ease their pain. Then I suggested we give Muttley an immediate funeral and got them busily involved in the arrangements. Sensitive Nannette suffered Muttley's loss the most. Through sobs and tears, she suggested that we mark Muttley's grave with a wooden cross. She helped me make a cross to mark his grave and keeping her siblings busy helped ease their pain.

We buried Muttley at the edge of the woods he loved to roam, beneath a small, white, wooden cross inscribed with the words: "In memory of Muttley who in his short life roamed these woods happy and free."

Sam seemed puzzled over the loss of Muttley, but his death did not dampen her enthusiasm for hunting and she enjoyed the extra attention she now received from 'her' kids.

Soon after the loss of Boots and Muttley, my wife and I decided Sam had fulfilled her motherly role and so while Sam was at the Vet's for shots, we had her spayed.

I have pointed out how much Sam loved to hunt but perhaps hunt is not the appropriate word to describe her excursions into the woods. Although she chased all the wild animals in our woods, she wouldn't hurt any of them. In fact, the woods creatures probably welcomed Sam as a great form of exercise and entertainment.

Although Sam had a fondness for hunting, her greatest love was our/her kids. When the kids went to school in the morning, she would sadly see them off. Each afternoon, she would sit patiently in our front yard waiting for that big yellow thing that brought them home. At first sight of the school bus coming down the road, she would quiver, shake and whine in eager anticipation. By the time the bus rolled to a stop in front of our house, Sam was jumping in the air, rolling on the ground and barking excitedly. Dog and kids would greet each other with kisses, hugs, laughter and barks. This joyous scene always made me smile, though through moist eyes, because it was such a complete outpouring of uninhibited love.

One afternoon, Sam did not meet her kids with her usual enthusiasm. She shook and whined as usual, but she just sat on her haunches sweeping the ground with her tail and she seemed to be waving a front paw at them. We soon discovered that the leg she was waving had a compound fracture, but that injury and accompanying pain did not prevent her from greeting her kids. The children worried over Sam while she slobbered them with kisses, all the way to the veterinarian. The Vet examined Sam and explained that she had probably stepped into a hole while running and that surgery was required to repair the damage. He explained that it would be necessary to insert a steel pin in the leg and set the leg in a cast. This treatment would be expensive with no guarantee that Sam would regain full use of the leg. Once again, we were faced with a decision about this dog's future. This time the decision was easy and unanimous. Sam had become a member of our family and gave so much love and joy to us that we must help her. The leg was set and Samantha hobbled about the house on three legs while the bone slowly healed. The cast and steel pin were certainly an uncomfortable, cumbersome burden, but she hobbled about without complaint. After three months the cast was removed and we were delighted to see Sam had regained full mobility without a noticeable limp.

Sam was a member of our family for six years. She gave six years of happiness to our children and she was happiest when with them. Her departure from our world was unanticipated, as her arrival into it had been. It came at a moment when kids and dog were happily playing together. A moment that will remain imprinted in my memory for life.

It was Veteran's Day, November 11, 1980, just one year and five days before the birth of our fifth child, Kelly. Because it was a holiday, the children were out of school. My wife, a registered nurse, was at work in a nursing home, and Patrick, now 17 years old, was at work in a local restaurant. Our remaining three teenage children were raking leaves in the front yard, while I was busy painting our living room ceiling. The children raked the leaves onto a large sheet of plastic, which, when filled, they carried across the road and dumped in alder bushes. Sam was helping 'her' kids by grabbing at rake handles and rolling in the leaves. I painted on, with ears tuned to the joyful scene outside. Suddenly, the laughter was replaced by screams and crying! I rushed outside and saw a car stopped on the road at the entrance to our driveway. I fought personal panic as I gathered in the situation. My three kids and a woman, who I recognized as a neighbor, were sobbing over Sam who was lying on her stomach in the road. Realizing that Sam had been hit by our neighbor's car, I ran to them and prayed that Sam was not seriously injured. The woman was in shock and my sobbing kids begged me to hurry and take Sam to the Vet. I examined Sam, and she struggled vainly to get on her feet. I started to lift her and she whined softly in obvious pain. I knew the Vet could not help Sam this time and struggled to hold back personal tears. At a loss for words, I weakly assured woman and children that everything would be okay, when in fact I knew it wasn't. Sam had been hit hard. She was bleeding from severe internal injury and a broken back. All I could do was sit there stroking Sam's head and search her eyes for understanding of my helplessness. Even in suffering, those soft brown eyes radiated love. She stopped whining and her eyes seemed to smile at me transmitting the message, "It is okay, I am happy. I have had a good life. I love you all and I am at peace." Then she was gone! I felt like someone had hit me in the chest with a sledge hammer and stopped my heart. No longer able to hold back tears, but knowing I had to take control of the situation, I fought to gain composure. Wiping at the tears flowing from my eyes, I explained to my sobbing children how Sam told me she was at peace and wanted them to remember her with happiness. It helped, but not much.

I explained that we would have an immediate funeral and bury Sam next to Muttley. Then I directed them to gather the items necessary for the funeral. A box lined with blankets would serve as Sam's coffin. A shovel was needed to dig the grave. Pieces of wood were needed to cut and form into a cross. Keeping them busy helped ease their pain and suffering. We were soon gathered at grave side for the funeral. Overall, the children handled their shock and grief extremely well, although no one, including myself, could hold back tears. Poor Nannette, she kissed Sam and soaked her fur with tears until the brief service was over. Our eulogy and prayers were short, but full of meaning. I do not recall precisely what I said, but know what I felt in my heart. My heart said, "Samantha, it is true that you were only a mutt, but you possessed the grace, intelligence and elegance of a thoroughbred and your greatest attribute was complete and unconditional love. Our family has been truly blessed by the gift of your love."

We buried Samantha on the edge of the woods she loved, beside the puppy she loved, at the foot of a white wood cross simply inscribed, 'Sam-antha.'

SHORTS THAT FIT WELL

GUARDIAN ANGEL

Katie O'Malley was five years old and she was mad! "Why did God have to make boys," she sputtered to her mother. "Timmy is always so mean Momma. Why don't you give him away?"

"Now Katie," Kathleen O'Malley replied, "Timmy is your brother and although he picks on you and makes you angry, I am sure he loves you in his heart. Today at Mass, I want you to pray for Timmy and I will have him confess the breaking of your music box to Father O'Brien. I will also withhold money from his allowance until there is enough to buy you another music box."

"But momma," Katie sobbed – tears flowing down freckled cheeks as she complained – "Odette was a very special ballerina and we will never be able to replace her."

Odette was the tiny porcelain ballerina atop a music box that played the theme from Swan Lake Ballet. Aunt Sarah, Katie's favorite aunt, had purchased the music box in the gift shop at Lincoln Center Performing Arts in Manhattan, immediately after they attended the beautiful ballet, Swan Lake. Now sadly, Aunt Sarah was very sick and in danger of dying, Timmy had broken Aunt Sarah's precious gift and Katie felt miserable.

It was a cool, cloudy Sunday, and Katie was in no mood to leave home. She just wanted to stay in her room where she could pout and cry. However, mother insisted that going to church would make her feel better and she could pray at Mass for Jesus to heal Aunt Sarah. "But momma," she protested, "Daddy said he is not going to Mass with us. I could stay home and pray in my room."

"Your father went to Mass last night," mother replied. He has something he needs to do today and your prayers will be better heard in the house of our Lord."

"But momma," Katie protested with tear filled eyes, "I am so mad at Timmy I can't pray, and besides, God is mean to let Aunt Sarah get sick when he knows how much I love her."

"Hush what you say child!" Mrs. O'Malley gently rebuked, "God does not cause sickness. He loves us! Life is always an uncertainty. We make of it what we will and if we love God, obey his laws, and live a good life, we pass on to eternal life with him in Heaven. We cannot choose that day, and some enter Heaven at a younger age than others."

Katie's heart was aching and her mother's words were not easing her pain. "But momma," she protested, "why Aunt Sarah? She is my favoritist (sic) person in the world."

Katie lived in Ticonderoga, New York, a small, but bustling community located in the shadow of New York's Adirondack Mountains. She was about to graduate from kindergarten at Saint Mary's School, and eagerly looked forward to starting first grade because her teacher would be Mrs. Millificent, who had a neat sounding name and possessed a wonderful smile. Katie had red chestnut hair – normally worn in braided pigtails – large blue eyes, and her rosy cheeks were dotted with freckles. At first glance, one would rightfully assume she was an Irish lass, and the name O'Malley, lent credence to that suspicion. Her father, Patrick O'Malley, was fourth generation O'Malley, proudly named after his grandfather. However, breaking with family tradition, Patrick named his first born, Timothy. Kathleen O'Malley's maiden name was Ryan and she was as Irish as her husband. Patrick O'Malley was tall, had dark curly hair, a square chin and to daughter Katie, was the handsomest man in the world. Kathleen had thick chestnut red, curly hair, sparkling blue eyes, a pale complexion, with just a dash of freckles, and normally a smile lent attractive quality to her lovely face. Katie believed her mother was the second most beautiful woman in the world. The first, was her mother's sister, Sarah, who Katie absolutely adored; likely, because Aunt Sarah, who was single and lived alone, doted on her little niece.

While waiting for mother to finish getting ready for church, Katie studied her broken music box and reflected on the happy day it came into her possession. Aunt Sarah had purchased the tickets for the ballet and also tickets to travel by train to New York City. This was Katie's first trip to the city which her dad referred to as, "The Big Apple," and upon entering the bustling metropolis she wondered how anyone could liken this world of concrete, huge buildings, traffic, masses of people and so much noise, to an apple. Mother had told her that she must not stray from her while they were in New York, but she needn't have worried about that. Katie was intimidated and frightened by the masses of people. She walked between mother and Aunt Sarah, gripping their hands tightly. After they entered Lincoln Center and found their seats – which were only ten rows back from the orchestra pit – Katie began to relax and examine her surroundings. She was awestruck by the beauty, magnificence and size of the theater and estimated it would hold a gazillion people. Of course she didn't know how many were required to make a gazillion, but that was the largest number she could relate to. Aunt Sarah told Katie that she knew one of the violin players in the orchestra and when she saw her friend enter the orchestra pit, she took Katie up and introduced her to Michelle Owens. Michelle had long dark hair, which hung loosely down her back and wore a dark, low bodice, short sleeve dress. She had dark, expressive eyes and other than a single strand of small pearls around her neck, wore no other jewelry. Katie thought Michelle was beautiful, but not quite as beautiful as Aunt Sarah or her mother. Michelle and Aunt Sarah conversed for a moment and then they returned to their seats. Katie was thrilled that Michelle had let her examine her violin.

Katie remained in awe of everything around her, but the introduction to Michelle was thrilling and put her at ease. She was beginning to really enjoy this magnificent theater and her big blue eyes glowed with excitement and anticipation. She studied the people arriving to attend the performance and marveled at their elegant dress. Now she knew why her mother made her wear her very best orchid, taffeta dress and had labored to twist her thick chestnut hair into a French twist.

Katie stared upward in wide-eyed amazement as huge golden chandelier lights dimmed and at the same time seemed to disappear into the ceiling. While trying to comprehend this mystery, the sound of music drew her attention toward the stage. The orchestra began to play and the massive curtains fronting the stage parted, revealing a beautiful moonlit forest glade. Suddenly, the most graceful people she had ever seen magically appeared. They didn't walk or run onto the stage, but flowed onto it in rhythm with the music. It seemed to Katie that she was having a dream, yet she knew she was awake and the dancers flowing on the stage were real people. By intermission, Katie had decided that she wanted to become a ballerina and someday dance in this beautiful place. Mother had told her the story being portrayed would be very sad, but Katie was spell struck by the grace and beauty of the performance. In her young mind she imagined that Odette and Prince Siegfried found peace in Heaven. At the conclusion of the performance, Katie rose to her feet and clapped as hard as her small hands would permit through encore after encore. The more exciting encore came when Aunt Sarah led them into the crowded gift shop and purchased the beautiful music box with Odette poised on her toes atop the box. It immediately became Katie's most prized possession. She kept the music box on a shelf over the head of her bed, only allowing the music to play and Odette dance for special friends.

Yesterday, Timmy, without invitation or warning, entered her room and threw his Nerf ball at her. The Nerf ball – which supposedly wouldn't hurt anything – struck Odette and knocked the music box off its shelf. During its fall to the floor, the box struck a bedpost, which detached Odette from the top. Sensing he was in trouble, Timmy ran from her room. Katie retrieved Odette from the carpeted floor, examined her and found that other than having been separated from the music box, she was intact. She clutched Odette against her breast and began quietly sobbing. Her heart was broken! Gathering strength, she continued to clutch Odette to her heart and sought out mother. She wandered into her parent's bedroom and found mother lying face down across her bed. *Why was she crying too?* Continuing to clutch Odette in one tiny hand, she joined her mother on the bed. They embraced each other and cried together.

"Oh momma," Katie moaned, "Timmy is so awful. I am sorry he made you cry too."

Mother responded by kissing her on the forehead and attempted to force a smile made wet by the tears that flowed down her cheeks. Then she ran her fingers through Katie's hair as she replied, "Oh Katie, my dear sweet little girl. Timmy did not cause my tears. My heart is saddened because my sister – your Aunt Sarah – who as you know has been sick with cancer, has learned that she may not be with us much longer. We must pray for her Katie, my dear."

Mother's words sent a shock wave through Katie's already wounded heart! She moaned, "No momma! No! It can't be! I just saw Aunt Sarah last week and she told me she felt that her treatment was helping and she was improving."

"I'm sorry Katie," mother softly replied. "I know you love Aunt Sarah and she loves you. She did not want to worry you, so she didn't tell you of her latest diagnosis. The only reason I am telling you now, is to have you add your prayers to mine. Dear Jesus pays special heed to prayer from innocent children and we must ask him to please hear us and heal Sarah."

A stream of tears now flowed down Katie's freckled cheeks and she moaned in reply, "I will Mother, and I will pray to my guardian angel too."

Mother and daughter then clutched each other and cried until they found solace and strength in each other's embrace.

The O'Malley's were parishioners of Saint Mary's, which had been the family church for decades, and Father Gerard O'Brien, possessing the smile and impish behavior of a leprechaun, was their pastor.

Katie always saw her guardian angel when she went to church because (in her mind), he lived in a beautiful stained glass window on the left side of the church overlooking the fourth pew from the altar. The O'Malley family always tried to arrive at Mass early so that they could sit in what many parishioners referred to as, "The O'Malley family pew." Katie was also sure that her guardian angel was Great Grandfather Patrick J. O'Malley, because the inscription at the bottom of the window – in large Gothic lettering – proclaimed, "In Memory of Patrick J. O'Malley." The window was quite large and its multi-colored, carefully placed, small glass panes, depicted a thin, gaunt faced Jesus, garbed in white robe and sandals, holding a lamb in his arms. Jesus was portrayed with large, dark, staring, expressionless eyes as he gazed down upon the congregation. Katie had never been told that the man portrayed in the window was Jesus, and therefore assumed the image was that of her Great Grandfather. The mistaken identity was partly due to an incident that occurred when she was 4-years old. Normally, Katie sat between her mother and father at Mass, and Timmy, sat on the right side of father. That day, both children were seated next to each other between their parents and Timmy kept turning toward Katie and making mean faces. She loudly protested, "Mommy, make him stop it!"

Mother had scowled at both of them, pointed up at the window and whispered, "Be good now, 'He' is watching you."

Katie had seen the man in the window before that day, but mother's words caused her to focus on and study the Angel in the window. The Angel stared back at her and his intense, dour look, made her embarrassed and ashamed. Though only four, she recognized that the letters on the window spelled the name Patrick J. O'Malley, and therefore assumed the Angel in the window was her great grandfather. Her young mind reckoned, *must be great Grandpa O'Malley is my Guardian Angel.* From that day on, an awestruck Katie, was careful not to misbehave in church. She frequently looked up at the window to see if Grandpa O'Malley was watching her. It seemed he always was which concerned her greatly, because he never smiled and was always so serious. *Perhaps great Grandpa O'Malley didn't get much to eat she reasoned,* as she studied the Angel's gaunt face and thin body. *Maybe being hungry is what makes him look so serious and unhappy. I have heard Daddy say that times were tough back in the old days.* She also reasoned, *great Grandpa must have raised sheep because he is holding a lamb in his arms.* The Angel's dress of robe and sandals inspired her to think, *Grandpa sure wore funny clothes. Maybe he wore a nightshirt all the time because he didn't have money for clothes and shoes.* Katie frequently prayed to great Grandpa Guardian Angel; was careful to always be polite and always ended her prayers for assistance with, "Thank you! I hope you are getting enough to eat in Heaven and I promise to try and be good." Now, on a cloudy Sunday, in the spring of her 5th year of life, Katie was confused, depressed and angry. Aunt Sarah was horribly sick and her special gift to Katie, the beautiful Odette, was broken. On the way to church she silently invoked, *I hope Grandpa O'Malley has had enough to eat today and is in a listening mood. I know Momma says Heaven is a beautiful special place, but Aunt Sarah is too young to go there. Besides, I can't bear to live without her.*

Rain threatened and large billowing clouds hid the sun. The ominous weather almost seemed appropriate for the darkness and depression mother and daughter were feeling as they entered the church. They proceeded to the family pew and genuflected before taking their seat. Katie glanced up at the window as she took her place beside mother in the pew. Grandpa O'Malley stared back at her and his face displayed the familiar dour, hungry look, which deepened the ache in Katie's heart. She started crying softly.

Mother gave her a tissue to wipe away the tears, placed her arm around Katie's shoulder and whispered in her ear, "It's okay to cry Katie. It will make you feel better and maybe attract compassion from Jesus."

Not wanting anyone around her to see her crying, Katie knelt on the kneeling rail, put her face in her hands and prayed harder than she had ever prayed before. She silently prayed: *Please, oh please, great Grandpa Angel, talk to God and ask him to please let Aunt Sarah get better. I know Aunt Sarah would like Heaven and be a wonderful Angel, but I would miss her so much. Please let Aunt Sarah live, at least till I am grown up, and I promise that when I get to Heaven I will help you get enough to eat. I will also help you watch your sheep so you can rest and be happy. Great Grandpa Angel, I was going to ask you to punish Timmy for breaking Odette, but* (choking back sobs) *Aunt Sarah is more important than an old music box. So, I will forgive Timmy and* (deeper sobs) *put Odette away, if you will help make Aunt Sarah better.* Tears now streamed down her face, and her concluding *"Thank you,"* was barely distinguishable.

Mother had not heard Katie's silent prayer, but she recognized her daughter's emotional pain. She put her arm around Katie and drew her sobbing little daughter's head against her breast.

While Katie was praying, a rising warm breeze blew the clouds away and a bright sun now bathed the interior of the church with warm sunlight.

Mass was nearly over before Katie lifted her head and took a quick peek at her Guardian Angel through fingers hiding her eyes. Her eyes and mouth opened wide in amazement! *Great Grandpa must have heard my prayers!* Her Guardian Angel was smiling at her and the ray of sparkling light from his eyes transmitted a silent message of warmth and assurance. "Thank you Grandpa Angel," she whispered aloud in awe.

"What did you say Katie," mother asked?

Katie smiled at her mother and replied, "I was just thanking my Guardian Angel for making Aunt Sarah better."

Mrs. O'Malley was not sure what to make of the sudden change that came over her daughter, but was thankful for her apparent recovery.

As they left the church parking lot, Mrs. O'Malley mentioned to Katie that she was glad she was feeling better.

"You will feel better too Momma," Katie responded cheerily. "Aunt Sarah's sickness is going away and we will be happy again."

"Now Katie darlin'," mother replied with concern, "I am glad that you are happy again, but Sarah is very sick and we must continue to pray for her."

"Oh, I will pray for her Momma, but she is going to get better 'cause my Guardian Angel told me so."

Not wanting to dampen Katie's new found enthusiasm, Mrs. O'Malley changed the subject.

When they arrived home from Mass, Katie ran into the house and gave her father a big hug and kiss. Then she bounded into her room to tell Odette the news. Odette was not on the dresser top where she had left her! She glanced frantically around the room and momentarily felt panic. That panic quickly dissipated and was replaced by joy when she spied Odette poised on her toes atop the music box, which was back on the shelf above her bed. An awestruck Katie carefully examined the music box and found Odette firmly attached. She wound the key on the back of the box and thrilled as Odette performed pirouettes to the Swan

Lake score. Excited and happy, she carefully carried the music box and searched for mother to share her happiness with her. She found mother in her bedroom and she was talking on the telephone.

"Oh Sarah," she heard her mother joyfully exclaim. "What wonderful news. Katie is here now and she will be thrilled to hear this." Mother lowered the telephone from her ear and turned to Katie. She exhibited a wonderful smile. "Guess what Katie," she glowed, "your Aunt Sarah is on the phone and she had received some wonderful news. Her cancer is in remission and it appears she will make a full recovery."

Katie smiled in response and replied, "Of course Mama! I knew Aunt Sarah would get better because my Guardian Angel told me that she would while we were at Mass this morning."

SHORTS THAT FIT WELL

THE PURPLE MARTINS

Clutching his ever-present mug of steaming hot coffee in one shaky hand, the old man stood on the deck of his home overlooking the lake. He stared across the surface of the water waiting to see what sort of spectacular color display he would enjoy with this mornings' rising sun. A pink glow gradually surrounded the ridge of mountains that served as sentinels on the eastern horizon, and the sky became a juxtaposition of variable hues of pink, gray, orange and blue.

Taking a sip from the mug, the old man sighed and said aloud, "God does such beautiful work."

The haunting cry of a loon searching for breakfast on the lake seemed to lend endorsement to his assertion.

As the sun inched its way above the Green Mountains, varying pink pastels were replaced by the clear blue of azure and the sun's radiant smile caused millions of sparkling diamonds to dance on the surface of the lake.

"It's going to be a hot one," the old man opined, "and the fish won't be biting today."

He turned his attention toward the bird tenement located on the edge of his lawn at lakeside. It troubled him that there was no sign of activity. *The Martins should be stirring by now and the adults out hunting for their little ones breakfast. What's this? The tenement appears to be empty!*

Just the previous evening the birdhouse had been a swarm of activity and the old man enjoyed his avian tenants show from the comfort of his deck. Thirty adult Martins occupied the bird tenement. Every morning and evening, the occupants were joined by an equal number of Martins from neighbor owned bird tenements in search of breakfast or dinner. The birds put on a show of avian skill as they soared, swooped and dove over the lake in pursuit of the insects that sated their appetite and that of their hungry babies.

The old man loved the Martins performances and studied the industrious birds through binoculars. He marveled at how each Martin swooped toward the birdhouse at break neck speed and came to an immediate stop on the little porch fronting their nest. As the adult swooped in for its landing, two or three wide open little mouths poked out of the nest opening and the parent Martin crammed insects into a selected baby's mouth. This scenario played out over and over again from early evening to near dusk. It was repeated again just after sunrise each morning and lasted till every appetite was sated.

The old man enjoyed the Martin post feeding social gatherings as much as their aerial acrobatics show. Adult Martins would gather on the porch fronting their nests and socialize with one another in a cacophony of trills, chirrups, peeps and squawks. The evening social rituals usually ended as darkness began to envelop the sky. One after another, the Martins left the conversation, entered their nests and retired for the night. At dawn, the ambitious, sociable birds exited their nests, exchanged greetings with neighbors, flexed their wings then soared into new day's light in search of breakfast. Insects were the Martins favorite and only cuisine, and there was always an abundant supply.

The old man smiled and opined, *they may live on my property rent free, but in return, they keep my property practically bug free and provide great entertainment.* Sighing, he reflected on how much his wife had loved the daily Martin performances. "Gosh, how I miss her," he said aloud, while studying the silent Martin house. He pulled a large red polka dot handkerchief out of a rear pocket and wiped away the tears that trickled down his cheeks. Continued reflection, produced more tears as he thought, *how much pleasure these graceful, beautiful, little birds have provided us over their many years of seasonal visits. She loved these birds more than me. We had 60 wonderful years of marriage and the last 20, were spent living on this beautiful lake. Over those years, we sat together on this deck – like young lovers – enjoying the Martins exquisite performances.* Though awash with tears, his recollection of particular moments of shared joy, lifted his spirit and produced a wet smile. Two years had passed since the Good Lord had called his wife to commence eternal life in Heaven. Though his heart ached for his lost love, the ever changing beauty of this lake – that his wife had dearly loved – and the colony of Purple Martins, helped combat his loneliness.

The couple had not been bird fanciers when they moved into the house on the west shore of Lake Champlain, and the southern plantation design, 16 nest, white bird house that came with the property had played no role in their decision to buy the property. It was the comfortable Shaker style, red cedar siding home; just the right size for retirement along with the magnificent vista of lake islands and Green Mountains of Vermont, that influenced the purchase. They knew nothing about Purple Martins and as they moved into their new home in November, the birdhouse was unoccupied. Their acquaintance and eventual love affair with the Martins began the following spring.

The old man chuckled in reflection as he recalled their surprise when the empty birdhouse suddenly became a hub of activity. One April morning the birdhouse the couple had virtually ignored was suddenly full of birds! "They didn't even ask about the rent," the old man (much younger then) remarked to his wife. "They just took possession like they own the place." And, it soon became apparent that they did.

Fascinated by the friendly, social behavior of their insect eating avian tenants, who conversed in bubbly chirps and trills, the couple purchased a bird nomenclature book. They were surprised to learn that Purple Martins were indigenous to most of North America. They had not seen Martins prior to moving into their home on Lake Champlain.

The book indicated that the Purple Martin belongs to the swallow family and having lived on farms during their youth the couple were both acquainted with barn swallows. They mutually agreed that the adult male Martin with his royal purple neck, back and wing feathers seemed more beautiful than barn swallows. They also agreed that the clannish Martins who resided in these multi-chambered bird tenements were much more sociable than their cousin barn swallows, who built mud and clay nests lined with straw in the rafters of barns.

They were amazed to learn that their Martin tenants wintered in South America and began the long trek south each year as soon as their young were able to fly. The Martins returned to the tenement in mid April each year, arriving well after Robins had made their appearance and they vacated the premises by mid-August.

The old man diligently cleaned the Martin tenement each fall and made occasional needed renovations consisting of repairing roof leaks and adding a coat of fresh paint. Then he and his wife looked longingly at the birdhouse throughout the winter and eagerly awaited the certain return of their chatty friends.

His study and observations of the Martins indicated that the Martins were monogamous and both parents fed and cared for their young and both performed nest chores.

The male was easily identified by the royal purple cloak of feathers that adorned his shoulders and the female by her lack of purple and gray breast. From mid-April to mid-August every year the birdhouse was an active community of Martins, building their nest, laying eggs, hatching them and then feeding the chicks till they could fly. The Martins put on their morning and evening aerial acrobatics followed by a porch stage performance. The show improved after the babies hatched, for the chicks voracious appetite increased the length of the daily aerial displays performed by the adults as they seized insects. In turn, the porch social hour decreased. The birds' morning and evening performances were continued day after day until the young Martins emerged from the protection of the nest, flexed their little wings and took flight. As soon as each family's young were able to fly, the family set off on their trek to South America.

The old man remained curious as to where in South America his tenants wintered, hoping that it was someplace safe, and where people cared for them as much as he. *I know it's a silly thought he mused, but it sure would be nice if I could communicate with them. How exciting it would be to listen to the many experiences and adventures of these western world travelers.*

It was the first week of August, in a summer that – although late arriving – was very nice. The temperature had exceeded 90 degrees only one day and because a breeze blew off the lake, even that day was pleasant. *Too early for them to have departed* the old man tried to convince himself as he gazed on the vacated tenement. *Why only yesterday, I watched a mother Martin feeding her baby. I can't imagine the little fellow learned to fly during the night.*

The old man carefully gripped the deck stairway railing and slowly descended the steps leading to the lawn. He shuffled across the expanse of lawn to the birdhouse. Then he realized that he would need a stepladder to examine the interior of the nests, as the birdhouse was approximately 8 feet above ground. He looked up at the house, studied it as best he could, and sensed that the Martins had departed. He had always accepted the Martins departure with positive optimism for he knew that they would return in the spring. It was different this time though, and he felt abandoned and alone.

"They were sure in a hurry to leave me this year," he said aloud in a sad whisper, sad not because the Martins were gone, but out of fear that he would not be around to greet them when they returned. He pulled the large red handkerchief from his pocket, used it to blow his nose then returned it to its pocket. Upon doing so, he slowly turned toward his home.

"Chirrup! Chirrup!"

That sounds like a Martin and it seems to be coming from the flower garden, he told himself.

"Chirrup! Chirrup!"

There it is again. I was not imagining it. There is a Martin in my flower garden!

A perennial flower garden lined the edge of the lawn and the south end of the garden was only about four feet from the base of the pole supporting the birdhouse The flower garden had been planted by the original owner of the property and had once been a beautiful, colorful profusion of three season flowers, but since his wife passed away, it contained more weeds than flowers from lack of attention. As the old man scanned the garden in search of the bird, he sighed and said aloud, "Pretty much gone to weeds now. My wife used to keep it looking so beautiful. A bird can hide itself real easy among that gnarl of weeds and flowers. Little fella probably fell off the nest porch and isn't able to fly."

Worried for the little bird's safety, the old man got down on his hands and knees with surprisingly little effort. He remained very still, waiting for the Martin to reveal its hiding place.

"Chirrup!"

There he is hiding in the grass at the bottom of that peony bush. He studied the little Martin, looking for any sign of injury. *He looks okay. I think he is just very frightened and lonely. Poor little bird, I hope your momma hasn't abandoned you; can't leave you down here because you'll get eaten for sure.*

The old man slowly reached beneath the peony bush and gently cupped a huge, gnarled hand around the Martin.

The little bird trembled from fear and loudly chirped a call for help.

Holding the young bird carefully in his hand, the old man tried to ease its fear with gentle encouragement. "It's okay little fella. I'm only trying to help you."

Trying to get back on his feet by pushing against the ground with only one hand proved difficult. With determined effort, he finally stood and took several deep breaths to ward off dizziness caused by the sudden change in equilibrium. When stable, he placed both hands around the Martin and examined it for injury. Deciding the little bird was only frightened and not injured he raised his hands above his head and placed the Martin on the porch of the birdhouse. He addressed the little bird softly, "Don't know which nest you belong in little fella, but at least you are back where you are safe for the time being. Now I'm worried that your parents have abandoned you."

The bird did not move and uttered no sound as he sat frozen from the shock of his frightening experience.

The old man shuffled across his lawn and slowly climbed the stairs leading to his deck. He looked at the birdhouse and saw that the young Martin remained very still on the nest porch. The old man entered his home, went into the kitchen and brewed a fresh pot of coffee. Hot, caffeine loaded coffee had aided in solving dilemmas throughout his lifetime and he needed to figure out what to do about the fate of the baby Martin. Holding mug of black coffee in one hand, binoculars in the other, he returned to the deck and sat down in a lounge chair. Sipping coffee, he focused the binoculars on the birdhouse and pondered the plight of the little Martin.

The Martin slowly recovered from shock and began to stir. Flexing its wings and testing them with a flutter, he started calling frantically for his mother, "Chirrup! Chirrup! Chirrup! He screamed in a tiny voice.

The little bird's plaintive cries pierced the old man's heart. *How lonely and frightened he must be.* Fighting back tears, he began to quietly pray, "Dear Lord, I know it may sound silly that this old coot is asking you to help a bird, but, this little fellow sprang from your creation and he needs help. He has been abandoned by his family and not being able to catch insects, he will surely die. I know you have a lot of serious problems to take care of, but, if you can help this little bird it would be greatly appreciated." He pulled the red handkerchief from the pocket that held it, used it to blow his nose and then dabbed at the tears that had commenced streaming down his cheeks. As he did so, he continued praying in silence. *I am such a weak–minded fool to worry so much over the fate of a bird Lord, but I love those Martins. They have provided me so much joy and this little guy is all alone and afraid. Please help him in any way you can Lord. Oh no! He must be growing weak. His cry is growing faint and it sounds like he is now calling 'shree, shree.' Wait a minute! That call is from another Martin!*

Suddenly, an adult Martin swooped onto the birdhouse porch.

With shaking hand, the old man focused his binoculars as best he could and saw that it was a female Martin and he watched as she stuffed insects into the baby's wide-open mouth. The sight produced a smile of relief. *I wonder where the mother bird was and why she came back"* Guess I'll never know the answer, but, if you had anything to do with it Lord, it is sure appreciated.

The old man was relieved, but he suddenly felt very tired. The traumatic experience had sapped his strength and he felt exhausted. *Guess I better go in and lie down awhile* he told himself. He started to rise from the chair just as the mother Martin soared out over the lake again on another insect gathering mission. Not wanting to miss her encore performance, he settled back into the deck chair. He reached for his ever-present mug of coffee, resting atop a small table beside the chair. Realizing the coffee had grown cold he left the mug on the table and focused his attention on the mother Martin. She was providing an astounding encore to her already wonderful performance.

The mother Martin soared, looped, dove and slapped the lake surface several times. When she had gathered a sufficient quantity of insects, she soared back toward the nest, but passed it by. The old man sat in stunned amazement as the Martin swooped to a landing on the tabletop and dropped her mouthful of bugs into the coffee mug. She stood atop the table for a moment, eyeing her child's benefactor, then, emitting a 'Chirrup,' she swooped off on another food gathering mission.

The old man sat frozen in bewildered amazement for several minutes then a smile appeared on his face as he regained his composure. He looked upward and said aloud, "Thank you God for helping my little friend!" He silently added, *after all these years, a Martin has communicated with me. I wish my wife had been here to see this, though somehow, I got a feeling she did.*

SHORTS
THAT
FIT WELL

JETHRO RETURNS
FROM WAR

On September 19, 1974, Marine Corporal Jethro Lee, looking quite sharp in his olive green uniform boarded the bus that would take him to Memphis, Tennessee. He slowly made his way down the center aisle searching for a comfortable seat. He found a section having two empty seats, stowed his duffel bag in the overhead compartment and settled his lean, lanky frame into one of the seats. After enduring a year of heat, bugs, snakes, bombs and bullets in a hell hole that went by the name of Vietnam, Jethro was eager to return home. For him, home was a place of peace and tranquility known as Jasper, Tennessee. Trying to get comfortable in the close quarters of seats was but a minor irritation to most passengers. However, the constant ache from a piece of shrapnel in Jethro's left hip caused him to favor keeping his weight on his right side as much as possible. Shortly after settling in, a young man appeared and settled into the seat beside Jethro. Jethro nodded a hello and apologized to his seat mate for squirming about in his seat to keep pressure off of his left side.

Jethro guessed the young man seated beside him was about 20-years old and a college fella because he had long, shoulder length hair, which was popular at the time.

His youthful seat companion raised one hand, with fingers displaying the peace sign commonly in use at the time. While giving the peace sign, the young fellow studied Jethro with a scowl readily recognizable on his face. The young man's scowl and his sign of peace seemed to conflict with each other.

Jethro guessed by the young man's demeanor that he was opposed to the Vietnam War, as was common with that age group, and was probably anti-military. Jethro had already experienced an episode of anti-war protestors demonstrating outside Oakland Naval Hospital, where he was treated for his wounds.

Having studied his seatmate, Jethro assumed they would not be engaging in much conversation, so he took a magazine from the pocket of the seat in front of him and started searching for an article that he might enjoy. He was quite surprised when the young fellow commenced immediate conversation by asking him a question. Actually, the question came out more as a statement than a question.

"Were you in Nam?" Not waiting for an answer, he added, "that purple ribbon you're wearing means you were wounded, doesn't it?"

Jethro placed the magazine on his lap, faced his seat mate, flashed him a smile and responded, "Yes Sir. I nearly lost my left leg and still carryin' some shrapnel in my hip."

His young inquisitor responded by studying the display of ribbons prominently displayed on the breast of Jethro's uniform shirt, then inquired, "What does that ribbon centered on top of the other ribbons signify?"

Jethro placed his finger on the ribbon as he responded, "This one?"

"Yeah, man, that one."

"That ribbon goes with the Silver Star medal," Jethro replied.

"Wow! Did you get that for killing a lot of people?"

Jethro winced, gave his hairy inquisitor a dead pan look and replied,

"Well, I had to kill a few, but actually, I got that one for saving lives, not killing."

Face displaying a sneer, the young man responded, "While you were in Nam, did it bother you to kill people or did it give you a thrill?"

This incendiary question touched a nerve, causing the muscles in Jethro's jaw to tighten as he pondered how to answer; or even whether to answer, his antagonist's question. He responded, "Sir, it do appear that you are tryin' to get me riled. If that be your intent, 'jes' go find yerself another sucker, cause I ain't in the mood to be hassled."

"I'm sorry," the young man responded (though still displaying a smirk). "I don't want to get a trained killer mad at me. Just curious as to how you feel about having sacrificed so dearly in a war that has no defined purpose or meaning. It must have been hell for you?"

Before responding, the decorated war hero stared out the bus window and studied a herd of cows peacefully grazing in a field alongside the highway. Then, he turned his head, studied his antagonist with a sober look and began, "Yes Sir! No question about it. War is hell! My papa and his papa afore him fought in unwinnable wars most of their lives. Though they 'preciated a victory now and then, the enemy was jes to numerous and smart to defeat. Both went to their graves without winnin' their wars and the enemy is still proliferatin'.

The Marine's words were confusing because the young man seated beside Jethro, was unaware of any war the United States was involved in that would have been waged over countless generations – especially one in which the enemy had not been defeated. He contemplated Jethro's words, pondered history and asked himself *what war could have possibly involved both father and son? Possibly the Civil War, but Jethro was much too young to have a father fighting in that war.* "I am very interested in learning about this war your father and grandfather fought in," he asked, his face now displaying a look of curiosity.

Purposely responding in a strong southern drawl, intending to make his questioner believe he was not well educated and possibly illiterate, Jethro responded, "Well, during his lifetime my grandpappy kilt about 200 of one a his enemies and prob'ly a few hundred of tuther. My pappy kilt an equal number and still they kept a comin'. Jes too many of them and they was too smart."

As the young man listened his face assumed a look of amazement and his eyes now displayed an, 'I want to hear more look.' He responded, "Perhaps I should tell you that I am a reporter for 'Students Opposed to War' magazine. Our readers would definitely love to learn about your family war experiences. Your grandfather and father must also have been much decorated heroes?"

"Naw, neither one of em got any medals," Jethro responded.

"That seems incredible! Why weren't they recognized for their sacrifice?"

"Well, it wasn't a big deal at the time and nobody knowed or cared."

"How could anyone not be interested in war that involved the death of so many? There would have been many bodies to bury and families emotionally devastated by loss. Someone had to know?"

"Nope, weren't any buryin' necessary, 'cause they ate em!"

Jethro's response totally shocked the young anti-war reporter. His mouth was now agape as he stared at his seatmate with a look of shock and disbelief. He responded, "They did what? Surely, you aren't trying to tell me that your grandfather and father were cannibals?"

"Nope, but they sure did prove that war is hell. No matter how hard they fought, no matter the strategies they used, they jes couldn't win."

Totally confused, the young reporter shook his head and responded, "All of what you just told me is very confusing. I received an A in history and consider myself knowledgeable about all the wars our country has engaged in. What war, or, wars did your father and grandfather fight?"

"Same war's that is still goin' on today," Jethro replied, displaying a gotcha smile. "They's known as the war agin dandelions and the war agin squirrels. Can't defeat em, but shucks, squirrels is tasty and folks in Jasper know how to make dandy Dandelion wine. Now that ya have your war story, I'm movin to another seat."

SHORTS THAT FIT WELL

A MEMORABLE 6TH GRADE EXPERIENCE

1949 would be my last year attending school in the Cortland New York, public school system. I was about to enter 6th grade and was looking forward to another banner year of receiving straight A's. Little did I realize that 6th grade would produce one of the most shocking and memorable events from my entire school experience.

To put readers in touch with public education in that era, I will point out that, The U.S. Department of Education was yet to be established. Our nation's public school systems were funded and overseen by the communities in which they were located. There were no free lunches for students, although students in kindergarten and first grade received a free container of orange juice and crackers as nourishment. The curriculum consisted mainly of the three R's and school discipline was via 'the hickory stick;' although as I recall, my 5th grade teacher, Mrs. Adams maintained discipline via her 'Board of Education, which hung on a hook attached to her desk.

While attending elementary school, I tried not to incur punishment and strived to please my teachers in every way possible.

During the summer of 1948, my parents learned that ongoing renovations on the elementary school would require my attending 6th grade in the basement of the Cortland High School. On the day following Labor Day, I reported for class and was shown to the class room, which was in the cellar of the high school. Readers might be shocked to learn that large heating pipes, resembling the arms of an octopus, and covered with ASBESTOS, filled the ceiling of the room. As I recall, these heating ducts were quite large in circumference and our students sat at their desks, no more than 5 feet beneath the pipes.

Prior to reporting for class, I had learned that my teacher would be Miss Avins, which was a cause for concern to many of my classmates, because Miss Avins had the reputation of being a stern disciplinarian. It did not take long for many of my classmates to learn Miss Avins came by her reputation honestly as her methods of disciplining students consisted of either smacking knuckles with a ruler, or, twisting an ear.

On my first day of school, when Miss Avins introduced herself to the class, I guessed she was 'really old' (probably about 50), short and stout (about 5'2" tall and 3' wide). Her head was topped by grey hair tied in a bun and the scariest thing about her, was she always had a serious look and didn't smile easily or often. In this era, Miss Avins, could be succinctly described as a female MMA fighter. After a couple of knuckle cracking or ear twisting sessions, unruly kids in our class carefully avoided incurring negative attention from Miss Avins. That is, except for a boy I will refer to as Donald.

In my introduction concerning the difference between public education in the 40's and public education today, I neglected to mention that kids who flunked a class, were held back and required to re-attend the class until they passed. To my knowledge, there was no summer school program, special needs programs or tutor assistance programs. Kids who repeatedly failed grades, usually quit school upon reaching age 16. Donald was 16 years old; and a rather large boy attending 6th grade with classmates who were 10 or 11 years old. Donald was known to be a bully and having this reputation, younger students avoided him and he only got to bully us when we went outside during our brief physical education program.

We were only a couple of weeks into the school year, when Donald started poking or pinching a female classmate seated near him. He was engaged in this action quite covertly, so I did not realize anything was going on until Miss Avins – who had walked to the rear of the classroom while we were reading, or writing – approached Donald from the rear, grabbed his ear and twisted it. Not about to accept this humiliating discipline, Donald jumped to his feet and punched Miss Avins, causing the entire class to go into apoplexy. Incredibly, the blow did not knock Miss Avins down! She placed some sort of hold on Donald and dragged him from the classroom, while he tried to punch and kick her. Somehow Miss Avins, got him outside the room, where the two began engaging in a serious fight. I stared open-mouthed watching punches being thrown and two bodies slamming into the classroom door.

I will also point out to readers that as our classroom was in the high school basement, the room was not equipped with intercom. Every 6th grader in the room was in a state of confusion and shock, especially me. I personally wondered if the big bully was going to seriously injure or kill Miss Avins! Eventually the brawl captured the attention of some other adult, who happened to be in the high school basement and the Principal and Vice Principal appeared. They wrestled Donald down and took him away.

Incredibly, Miss Avins reentered our classroom, dabbing at the blood pouring out of her nose with a handkerchief, and ignored an obviously swollen eye. She went to the front of the classroom and commenced teaching as if nothing had happened. Every student in the class, including me, sat in stunned silence, wondering how our teacher was so nonchalant over having just engaged in a brawl in which she was injured. That day, I came to the conclusion - as did all of my classmates - Miss Avins, was a very tough woman and we would be wise to avoid incurring her wrath.

Donald did not return to class and none of his classmates were sorry to see him gone. His legacy was having initiated and participated in one of the most unforgettable memories I have of school.

At the finish of my 6th grade school year, I left the Cortland public system, as our family moved to a farm. A much smaller school that went by the name of Moravia Central School would prove quite tame in comparison to the excitement of 6th grade.

I lost track of Miss Avins and wondered if she eventually retired from teaching, or whether she gave up teaching and became a professional fighter.

SHORTS THAT FIT WELL

MY PERSONAL EXPERIENCE WITH "JAWS"

After the movie "Jaws" was released, people seemed to be interested in personal experiences dealing with sharks. I decided to share with readers a very scary meeting I had with very large sharks.

While in the United States Navy, I completed a two-year tour of duty at Cubi Point Naval Air Station, Philippine Islands and was a member of the first contingent of personnel to report to the magnificent new military airbase.

In 1992, the United States Navy decommissioned Cubi Point NAS, and the Philippine government took control.

Cubi Point Naval Air Station was located at the entrance to Subic Bay, a very large bay on the island of Luzon, about 70 miles north of the Philippine capitol city, Manila. Cubi Point mostly served as a land facility for carrier based aircraft; however, during my tour of duty there, Cubi was monsoon season home base for a – top secret at the time, and pre Gary Powers being shot down over Russia – U2 squadron. Whoever designed Cubi Point was quite brilliant in locating an airbase adjacent to a ship repair facility.

Two years seems like a long time, but to a young farm boy from central New York State, they were fun-filled years with plenty of adventure and excitement. The following account details only one of the author's many memorable Philippine adventures.

It was a typical hot, humid, tropical day at Subic Bay. Starting the day as usual, I ate a quick breakfast in the chow hall then strolled down the already warm street towards San Miguel Point. The airfield had been carved out of the base of a mountain located on the south curvature of the bay and living, dining and recreation facilities for base support personnel were located on top of the mountain.

Our concrete barracks were not air-conditioned, but were cleverly designed with walls consisting of screening beneath louvered slats. The mountain top breezes flowed freely through the building when the louvered sides were open. A single macadam paved road granted access to the airfield and this road meandered through jungle that was alive with monkeys, brilliant birds and various interesting and colorful wildlife. Married base support personnel resided in elevated homes constructed out of bamboo and these homes were located along the road leading down the mountain. These homes gave the appearance of luxury living in tropical paradise, but I soon learned that all sorts of wildlife indigent to the island presented a continual nuisance to the residents of these homes. Monkeys were apparently the biggest challenge facing the residents of the fine looking homes, as they stole clothing from clothes lines and invaded living areas searching for food and items that fascinated them. They could be very destructive.

The City of Olongapo was located adjacent to the ship and aviation facilities that comprised Subic Bay shipyard and Cubi Point Air Station. Olongapo was probably just a small fishing village until the United States Navy discovered that the huge bay, surrounded by rugged mountains, would provide shelter from the South China Sea that was often churned into a maelstrom by typhoons, and would serve as an excellent haven to conduct ship repairs. The construction of a naval base attracted Filipinos eager to obtain work and improve their standard of living. In short order, the fishing village that consisted of a small cluster of bamboo homes, was transformed into a bustling city. In 1957, the majority of Olongapo's residents either worked in some sort of service capacity on the two U.S. operated naval bases, or worked in the many nightclubs and eateries that served off duty U.S. military personnel. Although most of the nightclubs lining Olongapo's main street, were quite attractive establishments, the majority of the city's residents lived in modest homes constructed out of sheets of tin or plywood and the most elegant residences were small, raised homes, constructed of bamboo and having a thatch or tin roof. Typical of most cities and towns bordering on military bases, prostitution was a major enterprise. Permanent base personnel referred to Olongapo as Sin City and opted to drink and seek entertainment in the base movie theatre, enlisted club, non-commissioned officer's club, or officer's club. Lovely young Filipina women competed mightily for employment in the base clubs, and their goal was to wed an American, so they could go to the United States. Many did.

Marines manned the base entrance and proper military identification, or in the case of civilian employees; identification issued by the U.S. Navy was required to gain entrance. A large sign posted near the entrance gate to the base fascinated me. This sign proclaimed: "Warning, there are 96 known species of reptiles on Luzon Island. ALL ARE DANGEROUS!" On one of my trips through the gate, the warning on the sign became vividly clear. As I was conversing with the Marine Corporal manning the gate, an elderly Filipino man carrying a bamboo-fishing pole approached us and he was quite excited. He pointed back toward the stream where he had been fishing and shouted something in Tagalog, the predominant language of the islands. I do not know if the Marine understood what the man was complaining about, but he accompanied him toward the nearby stream. I waited at the gate and watched the action. I saw the Marine aim his carbine and fire three shots in rapid succession. He returned to his post at the gate carrying a 7 foot, dead green Cobra snake that dangled from one hand. He explained that the fisherman got really excited when he saw the snake looking over his shoulder. I think if that had happened to me, I would have been more than just excited. I would have had to return to the barracks and change my pants. That incident made me a believer in the warning on the sign, and while in the Philippines, I never got the urge to venture into any jungle.

I have another snake story about the Philippines, but the adventure I am about to relate deals with sharks, not snakes.

I always enjoyed the walk down the mountain in the early morning hours, as the road meandering through the jungle was alive with brilliantly colored tropical birds and noisy, impish monkeys. The monkeys chattered and picked at each other like little children playing pranks. Banana, coconut, mango and papaya trees were in abundance along the way, providing food and missiles for the pesky monkeys. Through the whistling, singing and chatter of jungle life, I could hear the surf slapping at the beach below. Each wave sounded like a sudden rush of wind that had reached a point of exhaustion. The sound was music to my ears and, combined with the clean, fresh smell of salt water carried on the breeze, was invigorating and inviting. Only the occasional distant thunder of a jet engine being tested on the flight line marred the serene solitude of the tropical island setting.

Lifeguards, Jimenez, Tagu, Martine, and Lubao, whom I affectionately referred to as, 'Jimi, Tag, Marti and Lu,' greeted me on my arrival. These young men were muscular, naturally athletic, excellent swimmers and seemed to become fish when they entered the water. I considered myself to be an excellent swimmer; however, I could not compete with any of them in grace and style. These young men loved their work as lifeguards and though – for the most part – no older than I, their instinctive knowledge of swimming and diving gave them the edge as soon as we entered the water. I was their supervisor and had the position through a stroke of luck, for my rate at the time, was Airman 1st Class, and my job classification was in air-traffic control. After graduation from air-traffic control school in Olathe, Kansas, I was issued orders to report to Cubi Point Naval Air Station for assignment to base operations. When I deplaned at Cubi, I strolled into the operations building to the office of the Lieutenant Commander that supervised air operations. I read all the messages posted on a bulletin board, while waiting to see the Commander. One message posted by Special Services (recreation department) was an advertisement seeking a certified Water Safety Instructor or certified Senior Life Guard to supervise civilian lifeguards on the base's new beach. While attending aviation school in Norman, Oklahoma, rather than going into town on Liberty, I spent my free time at the pool and went through the training for Senior Life Saver certification. While attending air traffic control school in Olathe, Kansas, I received certification as a water safety instructor, so I possessed the qualifications asked for in the posting. I opted to stop into the office of Special Services before going to the office of Director of Air Operations. The department was supervised by a tall, lean, rugged-in-appearance, gray haired Chief Petty Officer. The numerous hash marks on the sleeve of his uniform blouse and array of ribbons on his breast were indications that he was a career sailor and probably had seen action in the Second World War. "How may I help you son," he asked?

I smiled in reply and answered, "Good morning Chief, I am reporting for duty here and read the notice posted on the bulletin board looking for a beach supervisor. I possess the qualifications, but I recently graduated from air-traffic control school and my orders direct that I report to operations."

At the time, Chief Petty Officers, especially those who had seen combat, were highly respected and although outranked by commissioned officers, most officers – especially young officers – gave them a great deal of respect.

The Chief wrinkled his brow, extended a gnarled hand toward me and said, "Let me see your orders."

I handed him the thick envelope containing my service jacket (personal record) as well as the written order that directed my assignment to Cubi Point Naval Air Station.

The Chief examined the contents, which contained certification as to my being a lifeguard and water safety instructor. Upon finding that certification, he smiled and said, "Bay-a" (most everyone mispronounces my name) "welcome to Cubi. After you get a bunk and settle in, report back here to me. Consider your orders changed. I will hold onto this file and clear your situation with 'Ops.' Tomorrow, I will show you the beach and introduce you to the group of civilians that will be working for you. They are fine young Filipinos, about your age, and you should hit it off just fine. Get a good night's sleep and report back here tomorrow at seven."

I left the Chief's office, somewhat confused and wondering if I would be in trouble for not reporting directly to the Operations officer. No handshake had occurred; however, that was not uncommon in the military of that era. I had to trust that the Chief swung a lot of weight and apparently he did, for I heard nothing from operations and was introduced to the beach and my workmates the following morning.

Jimenez, Tagu, Martine and Lubao, greeted me warmly and in studying them it appeared obvious that they were about my age (I was 19 at the time) and although not related, Tagu, Jimenez and Lubao so closely resembled each other they could have easily passed for brothers. All three had the thick, dark, coarse straight hair, broad nose and broad facial features common of most Filipinos. Although resembling each other in physical appearance, Jimi and Tag were shorter than Lu, who at five-nine or five-ten was about four or five inches shorter than me. Martine was lighter skinned, blessed with thick, dark, curly hair, an angular face, pointed nose and appeared to be of Hispanic extraction. Apparently his physical appearance resulted from Spanish ancestry, and in fact, the Philippine Islands had been a Spanish possession for many years. I would soon learn that they were all slightly older than I, and at 22, Lubao, (Lu), was the oldest, strongest and would prove to be the wisest of the group. He maintained order and guided Jimi, Tag and Marty's activities. We hit it off well immediately and this group of happy-go-lucky, carefree Filipinos made my short tenure on the beach one of the most enjoyable times in my life. Each of them had experienced the brutal Japanese occupation of the islands and greatly respected and admired the Americans who came to their rescue and drove the hated Japanese out. Each of them had lost their father during that dark time of occupation. They viewed America as some sort of paradise and like most of the Filipinos I encountered, longed to go to America. They all admired and respected me; however, Lu was more serious than his workmates and he peppered me with questions about America. Lu was also the strongest and best swimmer in our group and he spent many patient hours teaching me to swim gracefully and with ease.

Young men all, we were in excellent physical condition and normally began our day by swimming up and down the length of the beach four times. As the South China Sea was very salty, we normally wore eye goggles, or face mask, while swimming and I eventually became able to cope with the multiple stings we received from small jellyfish that were translucent and floated on the gentle surf as we swam.

On the day of this particular adventure, Lu challenged me to a footrace. It was decided we would run to an outcropping of stone that marked one end of the swimming beach and the finish line would be the lifeguard tower located in the center of the nearly quarter mile long beach. We dashed up the sandy beach and Lu quickly took the lead. It would prove hardly a contest, for this agile Filipino was much faster than me on land or in the water. He easily won the race. We paused for a moment to catch our breath and then dashed into the surf to complete our morning exercise.

After our swim, it was time for coffee. We ambled over to the "Officer's Hut," which was not yet open for business. I always brewed the coffee, having learned early on that these Filipinos thought good coffee was the texture of mud.

The officers hut was a large cabana with a combination restaurant, bar and lanai, located on that portion of the beach designated for exclusive use of commissioned officers and their families. It was situated in the innermost curve of a small lagoon. Standard military protocol in that era required separate facilities for officers and enlisted men. As supervisor of lifeguards, I was fortunate to partake of the amenities provided at the officer's cabana, but only in the morning before the arrival of officers or their family members.

Entering the lagoon that comprised that section of beach designated for officers and their family members from the enlisted men's beach could be compared to leaving a Long Island beach and stepping into a movie setting from "South Pacific." An outcropping of rocks separated the two beaches. In fact, many movie scenes had been filmed in this lagoon. Tall coconut palms clustered together and graced the beach of glistening golden sand. An off shore coral reef buffered the surf rolling toward shore from the open sea and by the time the surf reached this tiny cove, its power was spent and it gently kissed the shore. Brilliantly hued tropical birds filled the palms with color and song adding enchantment to the idyllic scene. I loved this section of beach most of all and spent the majority of my time there.

This particular day was occasionally cloudy and Lu was the first to note that even though there was only a light breeze, it seemed to change direction often. He predicted an early monsoon, which was a gloomy prediction indeed, for during the rainy season the beach was closed.

On days when there were few visitors to the beach, we would take our lifeguard boat out to the reef and spearfish, or dive for coral. The Filipinos ate whatever fish we got and we sold coral to the wives of service personnel for $2 per chunk. I would imagine that removing coral from the reef would be illegal today, but 60 years ago that restriction did not exist. The boys loved to dive for coral and seashells, as sales of these items supplemented their meager wages. Gathering coral and shells was an easy task, for the beach sloped gently out to the water and after entering the water, the bottom – depending on the tide – was sandy to a depth of about 8 feet. Approximately 200 yards off shore, the sand disappeared and the bottom became a myriad of color and teeming life. Coral of every size-shape and color covered the sea floor. Brilliant reds, bright blues, golden yellows and ivory whites, covered the bottom like an artistic jungle. The particular type of coral and its life stage apparently determined its coloring. The coral provided habitat and protection for a vast variety of marine life. Swimming above the reef could be compared to swimming in an endless aquarium containing a myriad of exotic and colorful sea creatures that darted about or lolled quietly in the forest of coral. Goldfish, angelfish, gar, seahorses, small octopi, soft shell crab, hard shell crab, sea turtles and rays of varying size glided above or hid among the coral. We frequently observed sea snakes, but they seemed quite timid and we never came in contact with them. We were careful when removing coral, because barracuda and eels lurked in crevices and could deliver a nasty bite.

The coral jungle stretched out toward the sea at an average depth of 10 thru 15 feet until suddenly, about 1000 yards off shore, the beautiful blue water – made blue by the sun filtering through shallow salt water – turned to murky darkness. This change in watercolor marked the edge of the reef. Here, as at cliff's edge, the bottom disappeared from sight and water depth was measured in fathoms, rather than feet. Large barracuda lurked in dark crevices and huge sharks patrolled along the reef edge searching and waiting for some hapless tidbit. As our dive gear consisted of swim fins and facemask with snorkel tube, we seldom ventured too close to reef's edge.

It had been a good season for us, which meant there were no drowning victims, no victim recoveries and no serious injuries. We only had to occasionally admonish drunken fleet sailors and marines for foolhardy behavior, but they were usually kept well under control by units of shore patrol, which accompanied large groups when they visited the beach. Our most annoying problem was the need to treat frequent burns the surf waders received from a nearly translucent ocean wayfarer known as jellyfish. Small, almost invisible jellyfish floated in on the surf and when they came in contact with human flesh, the result was a painful sting, comparable to a fire ant sting. Usually the pain quickly subsided and the victim was unscarred, except in memory.

I hated to see the season end, but I was not about to sit around dwelling on the sad prospect. I coaxed Lu and Tag to go spear fishing and we put out in our life saving boat with Tag manning the oars. Tag was 20-years old, lean, muscular and the best diver in our group. He spoke broken English and preferred to converse in Tagalog, the island dialect, which I was never able to master. Tag was generally quiet and shy in a group of people, but was uninhibited when we were alone. He rowed out about 200 yards, and as there were only two spear guns, he stayed in the boat, while Lu and I dropped overboard, each armed with a spear gun and small knife attached to our waist. We skimmed along the surface searching the bottom for a worthwhile prize. As our spear guns were cheap, small and spring fired, they were only effective against small fish at close range.

After searching for about ten minutes, a brilliant flash of orange caught my attention. Gliding below me, like a hawk soaring in the sky, was a small stingray. I was a hunter, and he was a hunter. We were both searching for a victim. He was a young ray; only about two feet from wingtip to wingtip and his whip-like tail appeared twice as long as his body. This was the closest I had ever been to a stingray and he was a beautiful, fascinating creature. His smooth back appeared to change from gray to blue and back to gray, as he gracefully flexed his wings.

Each upward motion of his wings revealed an underside of orange/white. Held in rapt fascination, I followed the ray for a long time with mind wrestling with conflicting thoughts; should I kill this eerie creature for its stinger trophy, or let him dwell in peace. The desire for attaining a stinger trophy eventually won out. I took careful aim, released the trigger on the spear gun and with a whoosh the spear struck my target. I was completely surprised when the spear passed completely through the ray's soft body and left it entangled in the spear's trailing line. The ray commenced a thrashing frenzy as it tried to free itself from the clutches of the line. In doing so, he created a cloud of turbulence on the bottom. I was confused. Now that I had speared my quarry, I didn't know how to retrieve it for fear of being stung. I looked for the boat and saw that it was a long distance off. However, Lu was nearby and he would know what to do. I waved to him and he swam over to me. When he saw the struggling ray, he became excited and asked if he could have it to eat, claiming it was a true delicacy. I assured him that all I wanted was the stinger and if he could subdue the thing, he was welcome to it. Without hesitation, Lu dove, grabbed the ray by its tail and with one deft stroke of his knife, severed it spine.

I was immediately relieved, but my relief was short lived. In my fascination with the ray and the excitement of the hunt, I had failed to notice that we were near the edge of the reef. The ray's throes had attracted unwelcome guests. SHARKS! Two huge sharks; dull gray, silent killers, 8-10 feet long, circled ominously around us. I had seen small sand sharks feeding along the shallows on many occasions, but these were the largest sharks I had ever seen, and their beady, black, emotionless eyes frightened me more than their size.

The beach was a long way off and Tag was 100-200 yards away, oblivious to our predicament. Short moments before, Lu and I had been the hunters and now we were the hunted! As the sharks circled around us, I came to the realization that they were more focused on the stingray than us, but we could very well become tasty morsels as well. The smaller of the two seemed the more aggressive and he eyed me, as a fish must ogle a worm before eating it, and in evaluating the risk of attack, he came closer and closer. I could have easily touched him as he circled around me, but dared not. At that moment, I knew fear such

45

as I had never known before. My pulse was racing and my heart was pounding as adrenaline surged through my body.

Lu had the only operable spear gun and it would be ridiculous to attempt spearing these monsters with a spring-powered spear, as they had Rhino thick hide. The spear would have as much effect as a spitball fired against a blackboard. As the sharks circled ever closer, the more aggressive one headed directly for Lu, who seemed very calm under the circumstances. I watched in horror, thinking, "My God, this is it!" However the shark only brushed Lu's body as he passed. Then, it made a half roll and eyeballed the stingray, which now dangled from Lu's hand. Lu dropped the ray, which still had the trailing line of the spear through its body, and we began swimming toward the boat. As the ray sank to the bottom, both of the demon fish went for it, appearing they would butt heads in their eagerness. I will never know if they did, for I was swimming as if propelled by a jet engine. Yet, that was the longest swim of my life, as I kept imagining the awful bump and searing pain of those demons ripping at my body. That bump and excruciating pain never came and I clambered into the boat unscathed. I needn't have worried about Lu, for as usual, he had beaten me. He helped pull me aboard. What a relief it was to feel the security of the boat deck under my feet. Physically exhausted, but on an emotional high, we chattered excitedly on the way to shore. I learned that Tag had nearly fallen asleep in the rocking boat and he had been oblivious of our situation.

It was two weeks before I regained enough confidence to begin diving again. I never did capture my stinger trophy; however, being alive more than compensated for that.

Jimi, Tag, Marti and Lu, commenced kidding me about going fishing and having the fish steal my spear gun, but I derived consolation in thinking one of those monster sharks might have eaten the weapon, gotten a severe case of indigestion and died.

SHORTS THAT FIT WELL

SUDDENLY A CELEBRITY

During my tour of duty in the Philippines, I frequently travelled to Manila, the island nation capitol when on liberty.

Virtually every visit to the bustling metropolis proved to be an exciting adventure. On my first visit to the city a jitney driver asked if I would be interested in visiting a radio studio to see a live performance by Eddie Mesa. Having no idea who Eddie Mesa was, I asked, "Is Eddie some sort of famous performer here?"

The Filipino jitney (open air taxi) driver spoke excellent English, and he was surprised that I did not know who Eddie Mesa was. He responded, "Do you like America's Elvis Presley?"

I answered, "of course. Elvis is very popular, and he is a magnificent performer."

My driver smiled and explained, "Eddie, is 'our' Elvis, and he is very popular, especially with our young people."

"I think I would enjoy seeing him perform," I responded. "Please drop me at the radio studio."

On arrival at the studio, I had second thoughts about seeing the show as there was a long line of people waiting to enter. I noted that most were teenagers and the majority of those in line were female. However, at 18, I was also a teenager and I might enjoy seeing Mesa perform. I took my place in line and felt uncomfortable as it became obvious I was suddenly the focus of attention. Studying those around me, I realized that I was the only American and happened to be the tallest person waiting in line. No one attempted to engage me in conversation and I did not attempt to converse with anyone. It appeared that they were talking about me but as they were conversing in Tagalog their native language, I had no idea what they were saying.

Upon entering the studio, an usher escorted me to an end seat in the first row. I thanked him and settled into my seat. Approximately five minutes before show time, the stage curtain parted revealing a handsome middle-aged Filipino, holding a guitar that was strapped over his shoulder. I presumed he was Mr. Mesa and this seemed obvious as the large orchestra seated behind him, rose to their feet. Mr. Mesa acknowledged the audience that filled the theater by waving, bowing and blowing kisses. When the whistles and cheers subsided, Mesa advised the audience – in Tagalog - to please remain silent when the "On Air" sign lighted.

I immediately recognized that Eddie Mesa was a talented, veteran performer, when the show went live over the radio. He opened the show with his 'apparent' theme song, and gave a credible imitation of Elvis. Enjoying the performance, I clapped and whistled loudly, when the studio sign flashed 'applause.'

At first station break, Eddie – speaking in English – announced: "I see there is an American present. I invite him to come on stage and introduce himself.

On hearing this, I turned around to study the 200 or so people gathered and did not see another person resembling an American.

An usher appeared, extended his hand and led me onto the stage. I was stunned, somewhat confused and developed the jitters. However, I went on stage where I was immediately greeted by Mr. Mesa with a smile and a handshake. He asked me my name, my age, where I was from in America, what brought me to the Philippines and did I enjoy

Elvis Presley. He also asked me how tall I was and wondered if I was a basketball player.

Mr. Mesa's warm reception and the positive response I received from the audience as I responded to the questions settled down my initial stage fright. I also knew that when the 'On Air' sign flashed on, I would be returning to my seat to enjoy the rest of the show.

The 'On Air' sign flashed on and Eddie surprised me by asking that I remain on stage. He then announced to his vast radio audience, that he was about to introduce a young American guest who would sing a number.

Shocked and surprised, I did not how to respond and stood staring at him.

Recognizing my nervousness, Eddie placed a hand on my shoulder, smiled and asked if I knew the words to any song popular at the time.

I responded, "I am a fan of Pat Boone, and know the lyrics to his recently released (hit song at the time), "Love Letters in the Sand."

"Super!" Eddie responded. He then had me introduce myself to his radio audience, flashed me a smile and said, "Give my orchestra the nod when you are ready."

I managed to sing "Love Letters in the Sand" giving my best imitation of Pat Boone, even including the stanza of whistling.

When I concluded, the studio audience rose to their feet and honored me with clapping, whistles and cheers.

Mr. Mesa, shook my hand and congratulated me with the words, "You have a magnificent voice. I wish you well in the future and hope you enjoy the rest of the show."

Then I returned to my seat and sat in numbness, reliving and pondering my experience. When the show concluded; while exiting the theater, I was mobbed by Filipino teens asking for my autograph.

Upon return to Cubi Point, I learned that several Filipino base employees, who adored Eddie Mesa, had heard me sing. They too, asked for my autograph.

The Eddie Mesa show would prove to be my only life experience performing on the air waves, and it was an experience I would never forget. Little did I know at the time, that approximately one year later, I would return to the stage to perform a much longer gig in front of a much larger audience. However, prior to that event I embarked on another adventure while on liberty in Manila.

When I travelled to Manila, I normally booked a room at the Manila Hotel. My motivation in staying there was the hotel was quite elegant, it had an Olympic size swimming pool, having three levels of dive boards, and most of the international airline flight crews stayed at the hotel, during their lay-over in Manila. Very lovely flight attendants (referred to as stewardesses at the time) were often gathered at pool side. The lovely ladies were friendly; however they were worldly, sophisticated and older than the somewhat bashful, teenage farm boy who ogled them. I didn't measure up to the standard they were seeking for a life-long mate.

One steamy, hot afternoon, I ambled into the USO club, which was located in the hotel. There was one other service member in the club when I entered and I joined him at a table. He was drinking a beer and I ordered a Coke. We took notice of the four young Filipino hostesses that greeted us and they thanked us for America saving their nation from the Japanese.

It would be appropriate to mention that after enlisting in the Navy, I stopped consuming alcoholic beverages, became a teetotaler and commenced working out on a daily basis.

Music filled the room, via records in a jukebox and one of the moderately attractive Filipina hostesses, possessing a lovely figure and delightful smile, introduced herself as Marla. She immediately asked me to dance. I thanked her for asking and responded that dancing with me would be an unpleasant experience as I was a klutz and would probably step on her toes.

Marla laughed and replied, "I happen to be a dance instructor and accustomed to Klutz's. She extended a delicate hand to me, which I accepted and led me onto the dance floor. After about five minutes of stiffness and struggle – while laughing aloud – she led me back to my table and took a seat beside me. During my association with Filipino workmates, I learned that Filipino's normally speak the truth and do not mince words. While holding my hand, she leveled her warm brown eyes on my blues and said, "You are a klutz. However, if you will let me, I will make you into a fine dancer. I would like to get to know you better and give you dance instruction. Will you let that happen?"

Her warmness and look of sincerity caused me to respond, "Yes."

I commenced frequent travel to Marla's home on liberty, where she patiently taught me not just dance, but the grace and style associated with various forms of dance. As Latin dance was very popular in the Philippines at the time, I first learned the Rumba. I next learned to Salsa. This was followed by the Cha-Cha, and we developed some very unique dancing maneuvers in each dance style.

In the hot, humid climate, I became soaked in sweat during our lengthy dance sessions. One day, when changing records on Marla's cabinet style record player, my hand froze to the arm on the player and my body was wracked by pain. Marla screamed at my plight. Recognizing I was undergoing electric shock, I barked, "Don't touch me! Unplug the record player!" Fortunately, she obeyed my instructions and neither of us was seriously injured.

Eventually, Marla informed me that I was a wonderful student and easily mastered the intricacies associated with each of the dance styles. Having mastered Rumba, Salsa and Cha-Cha, we tackled the Tango. I began taking Marla to Manila nightclubs. The clubs that we went to were high class, having orchestras. Most clubs in the city opened at 10 p.m. and closed at dawn. Though no Fred Astaire and Ginger Rogers, we danced to appreciative stares from other patrons. One of our nightclub visits produced a memorable experience.

We entered the club around 10:30 p.m. and after being shown to our table, we stepped onto the dance floor. I was attired in a 'Barong' shirt, (considered very dressy in the Philippines), black slacks and loafers. Marla was wearing a white Oriental sarong that accentuated her wonderful figure. The orchestra was magnificent and their focus was naturally on playing Latin dance music. We were enjoying the evening immensely.

At around midnight, a small group of people entered the club and their appearance, created a stir of excitement. Three young men escorted a woman to a table across the dance floor. Marla was excited. She put a hand on my arm, nodded toward the group across the dance floor and whispered, "That is Teresita Magsaysay, the President's daughter. Those men with her are probably body guards!"

I was aware that Ramon Magsaysay was President of the Philippines and was honored for being a hero during World War II. However, I knew nothing about his family and the presence of his daughter in the club, though notable, had little significance to me.

The orchestra was on break when the high profile group arrived, and Marla commenced telling me how revered President Magsaysay was.

When the orchestra returned from their break they commenced playing. Marla and I returned to the dance floor. Their first number was a very sensuous rumba. Their next was a cha-cha. We danced both numbers, then, returned to our table. Our focus returned to the group seated across the premises. One of the men suddenly arose from the table and walked directly to our table. The muscular young man focused his attention on me and spoke in a friendly tone. "Excuse me sir. Miss Magsaysay, requests the pleasure of dancing with you."

At a loss for words, I hesitated to respond. Marla was excited by the request and encouraged me to accept the dance request.

I do not recall verbally responding, but I followed the bodyguard across the floor and accepted the hand that Teresita extended to me. I escorted her onto the dance floor and our appearance caused other dancers to vacate it. The orchestra leader asked if we had a request and Teresita responded, "Besame Mucho' please."

Knowing that many eyes were focused on us, I was nervous and tense. However, Teresita melted into my arms and we flowed about the dance floor in rhythmic silence. When the number concluded, I continued to hold her hand as we acknowledged applause.

Dance concluded, I escorted Miss Magsaysay back to her table. She thanked me and we conversed briefly. She asked my name, my age and where I was from in America. She concluded conversation by informing me that I was very handsome and an excellent dancer. In awe, I flowed across the dance floor and returned to our table. Marla was very excited and pestered me as to my conversation with Miss Magsaysay.

I never saw Teresita Magsaysay again and we did not maintain contact with each other. Yet, how often does a 19-year old sailor, former farm boy from upstate New York receive an invitation to dance with a President's daughter. That chance meeting produced a most memorable experience.

Marla and I continued a friendly platonic only relationship

throughout the remainder of my time in the Philippines. It was a special time in my life and I greatly appreciated Marla's perseverance in building my self esteem. Typical of many Filipina women at the time, Marla was hoping that we would marry and I would take her to the United States. However, she was older than I and though I cared for her, I was not in love and had no interest in marriage. When I broke the news to her that my tour of duty was coming to an end and I was returning home, she wept softly and told me she would continue to treasure the memory of our time together.

My gig as supervisor of lifeguards on the beach ended with the arrival of Monsoon. As a tropical nation, the Philippine year consisted of just two seasons, Hot and Monsoon. During the hot season the sun and heat were relentless. It poured buckets during the Monsoon season and storms dumping ten inches or more of rain were common. I commenced working as a flight desk operator in the air terminal and upon gaining promotion to petty officer, commenced working as a tower controller. During my final year of duty, I was a shift supervisor in the air traffic control tower. It was great duty as the tower was air conditioned and the tower provided a magnificent vista of Subic Bay and the mountains that surrounded it.

The base Ops officer was non-demanding and easy to work for. Controllers had excellent working conditions and I appreciated a lot of free time. During my off hours I worked out in the base gym. I became a work-out fanatic and spent a lot of time in the gym. There was an additional incentive to visit the gym. A dance studio was located on a mezzanine that overlooked the gym area. The wife of a Navy Chief was the dance instructor and she happened to be a native of Hawaii, which wasn't a state at the time.

While working out in the gym, men ogled the women in the studio one level above and in all likelihood the women ogled the well conditioned men below. However, getting together was taboo. One morning, as I was finishing my workout, Helen (the dance instructor) leaned over the rail of the studio and called to me. She asked that I come up to the studio and move a desk for her. I climbed the stairs and upon reaching the studio, she immediately apologized for lying and displaying a pleading look said, "Next month is Armed Forces Day.

Our dancers are going to participate in a show honoring our military. I need a Master of Ceremonies to introduce each dance routine. I have been watching you and I would like you to be my MC.

I responded, "If I accept, what will I be expected to do?"

Helen was an attractive woman that I guessed to be in her 40's. Conditioned by dance, she had a trim figure and a most attractive feature was a warm, sincere smile. She responded, "As I will provide you the script for each introduction and dance routine, the only challenge will be, having to learn the correct pronunciation of Hawaiian names."

I studied her face and asked, "Why me?"

She laid a hand on my arm, leveled her brown eyes on me and responded, "You are tall, young, handsome, and I believe you have charismatic quality. Those qualities will contribute to our show's success."

Her praise won me over and I agreed. During the time leading up to the event, I studied my script and felt confident that I could handle the challenge and might even enjoy the gig.

A stage was constructed by our base Seabee squadron at one end of an open field located just outside our base. I would learn that the Marine Band, Philippine Symphony Orchestra, a Manila Ballet group, and Philippine Dance Studio would also participate in the show that day. The Marine Band would open the show playing a mix of patriotic and popular music. Our Cubi Point dance group would follow. When the day arrived, excitement reigned among all the performers waiting backstage. I waited with our dance group, gave the dancers courage and psyched myself that all would go well. I was dressed in a Rose colored Barong, topping white slacks and wearing white shoes. When our moment arrived, I stepped on stage, gulped and my knees started shaking. I gazed on a sea of humanity that filled the spectator area. I was later informed approximately 10,000 spectators attended the show. I mastered my best smile, took a deep breath and gave my introduction. After our dancers went on stage, I was thankful that all was going well and became pleased with my performance.

Every group of entertainers performed magnificently and I enjoyed meeting the performers. I took special delight in watching the Philippine National Dance troupe perform the dance, Tinikling.

Tinikling is a unique and unusual dance performed by four or more dancers. Two performers clutch the ends of long bamboo poles which they slap together in rhythm with music, while other dancers hop in and out of the slapping sticks.

Following the show, performers were treated to an elegant luau feast prepared by our Navy cooks. It was a very satisfying and memorable day.

Approximately two weeks after the show, I boarded the ship docked in Subic Bay that would take me to the States.

Now in old age, reflection on my youth, especially the adventures I was fortunate to partake in while in the Philippines, inspires a smile and I give thanks to God for providing me the experiences that boosted my self esteem and gave me pleasure.

SHORTS
THAT
FIT WELL

HE WAS A FORTY NINER

Dad was a workaholic! His idea of recreation was imitating Paul Bunyan, by wielding an axe, two-man crosscut saw, sledge hammer and wedges, to cut logs, firewood or fence posts. Virtually every weekend, Dad took older brother Bud and I to 'recreate' with him at the woodlot Dad had inherited from his father. My earliest memory of these outings was at five years of age. One Saturday, during the approximate forty-five minute drive from our home to the woodlot located on a dirt road in a place referred to by locals as "Nonesuch," (because none-such other place existed), Pa told me that it was time I started earning my keep. That day, he and Brother Bud were going to cut trees that they would convert into fence posts. After downing a tree, they would cut it into 8 foot lengths, which they would then split into posts. Pa explained that he would pay me a nickel for every post I dragged from the woods and placed in an open area by the road, where our car was parked. I was excited and started counting the fortune I would make that day. Of course, at five years of age, I had no concept of the strength required and effort involved to drag an 8 foot length of wood hundreds of yards.

After the first tree had been cut into sections, I managed to pick up one of the small logs and dragged it about two feet, before losing my hold on it. Pa smiled and encouraged me to not give up because he knew I could get that post down to the pile and I would make a lot of money. Over the course of the morning, I managed to lift, push, roll and drag two posts down to the lot. At noon, I joined Pa and Bud, for lunch, which we ate while seated on tree stumps in the woods. Pa had brought a basket of sandwiches; which had been prepared by Mom and a cooler of beer. By lunchtime, I was soaked in sweat and every muscle in my five year old body was on fire. I was dejected as I sat eating lunch, because my dream of making a fortune had become a nightmare. Recognizing my frustration, Pa handed me a beer and said, "Hey, cheer up! You have worked like a man and have earned a bonus. You can rest for the remainder of the day." I thought the bitter tasting beer was my bonus, but when we arrived home that evening, Pa gave me twenty-five cents.

Weekend after weekend, Pa, Bud and I, traveled to the woods and I came to enjoy those recreational outings. The woodlot consisted of a variety of trees and it amazed me at how knowledgeable Pa was about every type of wood and what it was best suited for. We frequently saw deer, pheasants, rabbits, squirrels, raccoon, fox and woodchucks. Birds sang sweet songs to us while we labored and I loved the serenity and peace of the forest. Of course during the winter, snow made traverse through the woods a hazardous adventure as exposed tree roots were covered with snow and slippery. I always looked forward to spring, as the forest floor became a proliferation of color. Wild flowers, mostly consisting of small purple lilies and Jack-in-the-Pulpit magically popped out of the ground, providing a colorful carpet. Over time, I learned to correctly pull one end of the crosscut saw and became able to split firewood. My muscles gradually hardened and by the time I was ten years old, I had little difficulty dragging lengths of wood that would be converted into fence posts, down to the clearing where they would be loaded onto the homemade trailer attached to our 1940 Plymouth sedan.

Nonesuch was actually named the Town of Sempronius, and it was the town of Pa's heritage. The Hamlet of Sempronius was so small, that while driving through the town, by the time you saw the sign announcing the township, you were already exiting it. As I recall, every resident in the township was either related or personally acquainted. Pa's woodlot was located about one mile from "Bear Swamp," which was a marshy area extending several miles, that teemed with wildlife and was a prime area for Deer hunters. Bear had been observed in Bear Swamp, although I never saw one, and it was said that Panthers prowled the Swamp and fed on white tail deer. I never saw a Panther either; however, several times I heard what sounded like the scream of a woman coming from the swamp and Pa told me it was the scream of a Bobcat. Never saw a Bobcat either; however, they were quite elusive.

There were few residents on the dirt road where Pa's woodlot was located. One resident was of great interest to me. He was a reclusive bachelor by the name of George Walters, who lived in a ramshackle wood frame home, having a dirt floor, just a hop, skip and a jump down the road from Pa's woodlot. According to Pa, George was a native who grew up in the hovel and his home also served as residence for the goats, geese and chickens that he raised for food and milk. There were no doors on the structure, instead, heavy blankets were attached to front and rear door lintels and hung down covering both entrances. The blankets were intended to block the cold of winter, keep unwanted insects out and 'hopefully' deter wild predators from trying to enter the home and feast on George's animals. I guessed that George was probably in his 50's or 60's at the time as he had thick grey hair, a thin build and his skin was withered. He was usually clad in bib overalls and two or more frayed sweatshirts. I wondered how George managed to stay warm in the winter, and learned the answer one Saturday in early fall, when Pa stopped to purchase a jug of hard apple cider. Though not appearing to be a wonderful farmer as concerns animals, George had a large apple orchard on his property, and he took meticulous care of his apple trees. Every fall, male residents of the township (women were repulsed by the condition of George and his property) visited George to purchase Cider and Applejack. According to Pa, George's Hard Cider and Applejack was better than any that could be purchased in a liquor store. On that Fall Saturday, on the way to the woodlot, Pa stopped at George's place to purchase some hooch and it was the first and only time I was in the hovel that was George's home. I noticed a huge potbelly woodstove located in the center of the premise and an unmade bed located only about 6-8 feet from the stove. Goats had greeted us outside the house on our arrival, and chickens roosted in various locations inside. Mom had baked a batch of cookies to give George and he was quite pleased with the gift. George led Pa to an area in the rear of the hovel which contained two oak barrels. I nearly gagged, when George spit out the cud of chewing tobacco in his mouth and then sucked on a siphon hose to siphon cider into the plastic gallon jug that Pa brought with him. After the jug was filled, Pa gave George some money, which seemed to be greatly appreciated. Then Pa shook George's hand and we departed for the woodlot. That is my vivid memory of George Walters, and in adult life, while passing by the location on the now macadam road, I wondered what became of George and how he ended life.

While at the woodlot, during beer and rest breaks, Pa often spoke of wanting to build a log cabin, in the same manner used by pioneers. Pa pointed out the location in the clearing where he intended to put the cabin and we came to realize he was serious about fulfilling his dream. In 1949, Pa staked out the plot of ground where the cabin was to be built. Pa and Bud commenced cutting the trees for the logs that would be used. Uncle Fred and I commenced digging the foundation for placement of the base logs.

As previously stated, Pa didn't own a lot of power tools or equipment, so I wondered how he was going to get the trees – of considerable size – down to the clearing where they would be cut into logs. That problem was solved when Pa hired a local resident who owned a team of mules, to skid the logs out of the woods. The mule skinner was a lithe, muscular man, who amazed me by his agility in moving and jumping out of the way of the trees the mule team hauled out of the woods, as the trees rolled and bounced along the forest floor. Pa and Bud, commenced cutting the trees into logs and that part of the tree that wasn't converted into logs, was placed in a pile for firewood. As they sawed logs with the crosscut saw, I piled brush and moved limbs onto a woodpile for later conversion into firewood.

Although having only a 6th grade education, Pa was an ambitious, intelligent man of many skills and talents. His primary source of employment was as a toolmaker in a machine shop. He was also a skilled carpenter and mason. In old age, he constructed colorful stone fireplaces in residences and established a woodshop in which he made furniture, toys and other items that were sold in gift shops throughout the Central New York region. However, that is another story. While constructing 'his' log cabin, he built huge sawbucks to place freshly cut logs on for peeling of their bark. How he convinced Mom to do that tiresome work is unknown, but I watched her using a two-handle draw shave to steadily peel bark from each log. As she labored, the log would be turned by Pa and Bud. Soon, Uncle Fred and Aunt Alida, began assisting in every phase of construction and Pa's dream of building a log cabin became a family project. After the base logs were in place, every log needed to be grooved at each end to permit locking in place. Pa measured and marked the area for each cut, then Brother Bud and Uncle Fred cut the grooves using buck saw and chisels. I do not recall the size of the planned log cabin; however, it was quite large and when finished contained two double bunk beds and furniture. It amazed me at how strong Pa, Bud, Uncle Fred and I were, as we lifted and fitted each log in place. Eventually the log walls climbed to 7 feet and it was time for a roof. I wondered how Pa was going to construct a thatch and mud roof and was pleased to see that he opted to purchase sheets of plywood and asbestos shingle for the roof. The final touch on cabin construction was sealing each of the log seams with mortar. I mixed concrete with a hoe in a square trough made by Pa and he pressed the cement into the seams with a trowel. Pa designed front and rear door openings in the cabin and he opted to purchase rustic looking doors from someplace.

Upon completion of the log cabin, Ma and Pa hosted family and friends at a celebration, smashing a bottle of bubbly against a corner of the cabin. Pa was pleased; however, his labor of love was not complete. What about water and toilet facilities? Dairy farmer, Lawrence Heath, with whom I would eventually work for and live with, attended the cabin celebration. He told Pa, he had an unused outhouse on his farm that Pa could have. A site behind the cabin was chosen for the two-hole outhouse and Uncle Fred and 11-year old Wayne dug the pit to set the outhouse on.

Pa was pleased to now have toilet facilities for his cabin and the charming little structure even had a half moon cut in its door. However, not pleased with its drab plain wood color, Pa, or Bud, (I forget which), painted the outhouse barn red.

Now it was time to set about the task of obtaining water and not having the money needed for a well driller, and still motivated to emulate the pioneers, Pa decided we would drill the well by hand. First, he invited a man he worked with who was proclaimed to be a diviner to use his talents in finding the spot where we would most likely find water. This process was quite fascinating to a wide-eyed 11-year old, who watched the young man, holding a small V shaped Willow branch in both hands, pointed end of the branch pointed straight upward, walk slowly across the ground. Suddenly, some sort of unseen force pulled the pointed end of the branch downward. When the pointed end of the branch pointed straight down at the surface of the ground, the diviner told Pa to drive a stake "here." He said, "You can drill right here and find water."

The Diviner appeared to be just an average Joe type human and I was mystified as to whether he possessed some sort of magical gift. When I asked him if he was a Witch man, he laughed and explained, "Nope, just a regular person who discovered the art of divining from another diviner." He explained that Willow trees always proliferate near water, as their roots demand a lot of water. He had me hold both hands in a palm upward position and placed the small Willow divining rod in my hands.

He instructed "Grip the stick tightly with both hands and keep the pointed end upward. Now walk slowly across the ground and wait for the magic to happen."

I shuffled slowly along gripping the stick with all my strength and was startled when suddenly some sort of unseen force pulled the pointed end of the stick downward in the same location where Pa had placed the stake. This was an awesome experience for a youngster always interested in learning life's mysteries.

Pa purchased lengths of steel well-pipe and we began the task of drilling a well via a sledge hammer and pipe wrench. This would prove to be a Herculean task, which involved Pa, Uncle Fred, Brother Bud and young Wayne in untold hours of toil, sweat and aching muscles. The first length of pipe to go into the ground had a pointed end and many holes drilled near the pointed end. A steel cap was placed on the other end. To start the process, the pipe was held by Uncle Fred and I while Pa and Bud, standing on step ladders began the drilling. Bud placed and held a piece of 2x4 wood plank, atop the pipe's cap and Pa smacked the board with the sledge hammer. The pointed end of the pipe commenced going into the ground averaging about a quarter inch with every blow. After the pipe started into the ground, Uncle Fred placed a large pipe wrench on the pipe. Following each blow on the pipe from the sledge, either Uncle Fred or I turned the pipe with the pipe wrench. Hour after hour, the labor continued every Saturday and Sunday, and the pipe went downward slowly. When Pa grew tired of swinging the sledge, Bud relieved him. After the top of the first pipe section was a couple of feet above ground, another section of pipe was added. The top of each pipe section was threaded, permitting a new threaded section of pipe to be added. Our labor continued for several weeks and Pa kept praying that the pipe's pointed end did not encounter impassable rock. Amazingly it didn't and when the pipe reached a depth of 96 feet, we heard a gurgling sound and water came shooting out of the pipe. Hurray!

Pa was jubilant when he screwed the well pump atop the pipe. Once again friends and neighbors were invited to celebrate. The log cabin now having water and an outhouse was livable and Pa could commence enjoying weekend recreation without having to drive to our home in the city.

Pa eventually added a kitchen and bathroom construction via regular studding and plywood to the cabin and the outhouse disappeared.

After the cabin had been converted into a livable home, Pa rented the place for a time eventually selling both cabin and woodlot when age began to take its toll.

Brother Bud and I never joined Pa in his elation over being what he referred to as "A Forty-niner" (not 1849 but 1949), by constructing a log home without the use of power equipment, and we failed to recognize that all that labor kept us physically fit and hardened our muscles.

Over the years, which involved a stint in the military and completion of two careers, I forgot about Pa's 1949 labor of love. Sixty-five years later, my wife and I decided to visit our old childhood haunts and we were amazed at how things had changed. The formerly dirt road that connected Bear Swamp and None Such, was now a paved highway. It was sad to see a vacant lot where George Walters had once shared a home with goats, geese and chickens. Gone too was George's magnificent apple orchard. However, Pa's labor of love, now a pleasant appearing cabin home, appearing to be well cared for, stood proud and strong on the corner of the woods, causing reflection on my youth and tears filled my eyes.

I realized that as a youngster and young man, I never fully appreciated my father. For years, I failed to recognize Pa's intelligence, his ambition, his physical and mental strength, his creative ability; how he appreciated nature and joy he found in helping others. That log cabin was a labor of love and he took pride in constructing it using the same methods utilized by the pioneers that shaped America.

Pa, you instilled your sons with ambition and drive to succeed. It took many years for Bud and I to realize that hard work and a desire to succeed, would achieve success and the "49er" log cabin project stands as a testament to your love for honoring the hard work of our ancestors who made America a strong and free nation.

RIP Dad! You earned it!

Claude Beyea of Moravia displays wares

SHORTS THAT FIT WELL

BAKED BEANS AND APPLE PIE

In "He Was a Forty Niner" readers were introduced to workaholic Claude Beyea. I now introduce you to Gertrude "Gertie" (to friends) Beyea, who was as ambitious and industrious as her husband, though their areas of industry and expertise were very different. Whereas, Pa was very talented and in many respects a creative genius as a toolmaker, carpenter, mason, woodsman and craftsman, Mom was an expert seamstress and chef.

Upon completion of 6th grade Gertrude Morris obtained employment as a domestic in the home of a well-to-do family in Syracuse, New York, which also employed a family chef. Though I am only guessing this is true, I believe the woman chef took the teenager under her wing and shared secret recipes that eventually resulted in Gertrude becoming an un-heralded Julia Child.

Where and how Mother learned her seamstress skill remains unknown; however, I would attest that she was an expert seamstress and the precious time she spent in a chair, with crochet hooks, or knitting needles virtually flying in her hands produced baby booties, baby hats, infant outfits, blankets, etc. that she gave to friends and relatives.

Mom was a dynamo of energy. Throughout most of her life, Monday thru Friday she worked as a seamstress in a corset company. On arrival home in the late afternoon, she prepared a tasty dinner for husband and children. Evenings would find her sitting in an easy chair crocheting while listening to the radio, and in later years watching television.

Every Saturday was laundry day. Doing the family laundry in that era required sorting dirty clothes, then placing them in an agitation laundry tub. Then the garments were run through a wringer powered by turning a handle. Then the freshly washed clothing was placed in a clothes basket, carried outside and hung on clothesline to dry. When dry, the clothes were brought inside for sorting. Garments requiring ironing were separated from those that could be folded. Frequently, depending on the weather, mom's laundry day ended at 10 or 11 at night.

Every Sunday morning Mother prepared a sumptuous breakfast for hungry husband and children. Sunday breakfast routinely consisted of either bacon or sausage, eggs, pan fried potatoes, French toast or pancakes washed down by orange juice and coffee. After the breakfast dishes were done (washed by hand in the kitchen sink), Mother enjoyed a cup of coffee while reading a 'True Romance' or 'Modern Romance' magazine, then, she donned her apron and magically (minus a chef's hat) morphed into a 'Le Magnifique' chef. Chef 'Gertie' routinely prepared a Sunday feast consisting of entree's such as: steak, (usually venison) pork roast, ham roast, southern fried chicken, beef stew, fried rabbit, fried squirrel and occasionally fried woodchuck. Entrees were preceded by tossed salad, potato soup, bean soup or pea soup, and included side dishes of macaroni and cheese, baked potato, baked beans and applesauce.

Every feast was topped off by one of her finest creations, which included: apple pie, custard pie, blackberry pie, pumpkin pie, mince pie, vanilla and cherry cake, chocolate cake, and infrequently, pineapple upside down cake.

Chef 'Gertie's' creations were not only tasty, they were large, as she enjoyed entertaining friends and relatives, whose taste buds apparently inspired a routine Sunday visit to the Beyea home. Visitors routinely and frequently uninvited appeared at our home on Sunday afternoon hoping to be invited to stay for dinner.

Two of Chef 'Gertie's' dishes became famous throughout the region, resulting in Mother being hounded for her 'secret recipes.' The two dishes were, "Gertie's baked beans" and "Gertie's apple pie." Um-um, reflection on both makes my mouth water.

Though pretending to be annoyed by folks pestering her for her 'secret recipes,' in truth, she enjoyed the attention and adulation. To each and every inquiry she responded, "I don't use recipes and I don't have recipes. I put in a pinch of this, a spoon of that, a cup of this and whatever herb or spice provides flavor," etc.

How Chef 'Gertie' learned and mastered culinary skill basically remained a secret, although she did inform inquirers that the important main ingredients in her two famous recipes were, 'navy beans' and 'Northern Spy apples."

Master Chef 'Gertie' is now in Heaven and I prefer to believe that if there is a kitchen in Heaven, Chef Gertie greatly pleases God with delicious baked beans and apple pie.

SHORTS THAT FIT WELL

A MEMORABLE CHRISTMAS

O'Henry's "The Gift of the Magi, the ironic Christmas story, portraying great self-sacrifice by Jim and Della, in the name of love, reminds me of a true life story of inspirational love, that had a twist of irony. Many years have passed since that Christmas; however, what transpired on that long ago day remains locked in my mind and inspires a smile.

Each year, on Christmas morning, family gathered in our living room, where adults savored coffee or tea and children hot cocoa with marshmallows, while my siblings and I, slowly emptied our Christmas stockings, to see what treats Santa had given to us. I thought Santa must have been under the impression I had a sweet tooth, because my stocking was usually filled with candy, gum, lifesavers, gumdrops, candy canes, cookies and or other edible treats. These were appreciated; however, the small matchbox vehicle, hidden in the toe of my stocking gave me the most joy.

It was a tradition in the Beyea household, that the distribution of gifts to family and friends, gathered in our living room to celebrate Christmas – rather than the typical helter-skelter everyone ripping open presents at the same time - would be a slow process. Presents would be distributed one at a time and everyone watched as the lucky recipient unwrapped his, or her gift. Then the gift was passed around for everyone to examine and the gift recipient showed their appreciation to the gift giver with a hug and verbal thanks.

When the children finished emptying their stockings of the gifts brought by Santa, it was time to distribute the beautifully wrapped gifts piled under our 'real' Christmas tree.

I was 10-years old, and this Christmas was especially exciting because I had been given the assignment of taking each package from beneath the tree, reading the 'To/From' label and handing the gift to the lucky recipient.

Our gathering that year included: Mother, Dad, Uncle Fred, Aunt Alida, my younger sister, Carol, age 4, older sister, Myrl, age 20, older brother, Ken, age 17, family friends, Roy and Eleanor Spaulding, and Myrl's boyfriend, Pat. Myrl and Pat had been dating for several months and my sister was madly in love with Pat, who was nearly ten years older than Myrl. I thought the tall, dark, ruggedly handsome, fellow having thick, wavy, dark hair, and face normally displaying a smile, was a cool guy. All I really knew about Pat was that he was a heavy equipment operator, who worked construction, owned his own home and seemed to have a lot of money. I also recognized that my father, who could be quite critical of "sluggards," (his term for folks who in his mind, were undesirable), had high regard for Myrl's ambitious, hardworking, boyfriend who knew how to handle money.

Sister Myrl, was employed (I believe at Smith-Corona Typewriter) and in that era probably made about 75 cents, or $1 per hour, and she paid Dad $15 per week, for room and board. In anticipation that Pat was going to surprise her with an engagement ring and pop the "will you marry me" question when she opened her gift, Myrl had purchased an expensive ring for Pat; a lovely ring that cost about two of her paychecks. She carefully wrapped the ring box and placed it in the branches of our Christmas tree.

Myrl and Pat sat next to each other on our living room sofa as we began the gift giving process. It was soon obvious that Myrl was excited and eager, for shortly into my distribution of gifts, she encouraged me to give Pat his present, and pointed out that it was the small beautifully wrapped item in the Christmas tree. I removed the gift from the tree and handed it to Pat. There was no need for me to announce who the package was for, nor who it was from, because Myrl had already made that obvious. As Pat examined the small package, he seemed nervous and his face turned red. By the time he un-wrapped the gift and examined the ring, his face was fire red. I thought he would be thrilled and embrace my sister when he saw the ring. That did not happen, and he mumbled an almost indistinguishable "thank you."

Having given Pat sister Myrl's gift, I thought it would be appropriate to locate Pat's gift to Myrl next, and found a carefully wrapped rectangular package under the tree. I read aloud the gift tag; "to Myrl, from Pat," then handed the package to Myrl. She did not attempt to conceal her excitement as she tore the wrapping from the package, revealing a shoe box. She paused for a moment, face displaying a look between confusion and curiosity. Finally, she convinced herself that Pat had attempted to surprise her by hiding her engagement ring in the box. The box contained a pair of slipper socks. Myrl, carefully searched the shoe box and then ran one hand inside each of the slipper socks, searching for the ring. As she searched frantically for the engagement ring, Pat's face was fire red with embarrassment and it was obvious he was ill at ease. Alas, the engagement ring that Myrl was confident she would receive was not there. She threw the slipper socks at me, and said, "Here Wayne, these won't fit me, you can have them, and her thanks to Pat was a look of disgust.

Pa, who appreciated morbid humor, struggled to stifle his laughter at the scene we had just witnessed and everyone else sat in stony silence.

I placed the slipper socks under the tree and decided it was time to continue the distribution of gifts.

Pat stayed for Christmas dinner that day and I thought that my sister's love for him would cause her to be gracious and grateful for her gift of slipper socks. Such was not the case. The look of adoring love that Myrl displayed to Pat, as I handed him his gift from her, was replaced by, first a look of dismay, and turned to a look of disgust when she opened her gift from him.

That Christmas Day, was the last time I saw Pat, and I always wondered what happened to him.

The slipper socks went unworn and eventually were given to a friend of Mother, who was very appreciative to receive them.

I know people love happy endings to a story and readers are now wondering why what took place on this Christmas, so many years ago, remains as one of my favorite recollections of Christmas. I would explain that the rapid change of emotional displays by Myrl and Pat, combined with the stony stares, confusion and silence from family and folks witnessing Myrl's confusion and anger; combined with Pat's embarrassment; followed by Pa's snicker, made a deep impression on an impressionable 10-year old.

Though this Christmas did not reveal the sort of indelible love shared by Jim and Della, the story does end on a somewhat ironic, happy note. The following year, Mother introduced Myrl to a tall, handsome, Korean War veteran, who captured her heart and who – equally smitten - popped the marriage question. They soon married and their marriage produced two wonderful children. They celebrated many joy-filled Christmas's together!

GOD WORKS IN MYSTERIOUS WAYS

Long ago, before the advent of computers, I-phones, I-pads, and even television, three five year old boys, Milton, Gregory and Wayne, resided in the same neighborhood. The three bonded together in friendship, normally getting together at Wayne's residence, as there were outbuildings on the property which were cool places to play in.

At the time war was raging in Europe, North Africa and the Pacific, and it seemed everyone in America was involved in the war effort, both spiritually and physically. The 5-year old boys contributed to the war effort by gathering milk weed pods and tinfoil, which were turned in by the boy's fathers to a war materials redemption center. The boys were told that the milk weed pods were used in life saving vests and the tinfoil was used in the production of multiple items used by the military.

Milton and Gregory lived next door to each other and Wayne lived a short distance away - just across a vacant field. The boys played together on a routine basis and influenced by the war, they usually played war games, fighting and destroying invisible Japs and Huns. Milton and Gregory's homes were small two story residences having a detached garage. These homes did not present as challenging a battle field as the numerous hiding places on Wayne's property, so their war games took place at Wayne's.

Although the boys homes were all located in a city, Wayne's home was located on the city line and was a small farm operation, consisting of two story home, detached barn, and chicken house, all of which provided cover for the enemy, which needed to be hunted down and destroyed. Another feature that attracted play at Wayne's, was a small stream which gently flowed along the property edge. The stream was home to frogs, turtles, polliwogs and snakes, which were fascinating creatures to them at their young age. They gathered polliwogs in jars and watched them mature into tadpoles, which were then released back into the stream.

Milton had one sibling, an older sister, who constantly complained about her little brother but, otherwise ignored him. Gregory had one sibling, a 3-year old sister, who adored her older brother. Wayne had three older siblings, who were busy in their own lives. They virtually ignored their little brother; except for Wayne's older brother who taught the boys how to gather and smoke corn silk. Gregory's mother infrequently visited her neighbor's and when she visited Wayne's mother, she brought her 3-year old daughter with her. Wayne despised Gregory's little sister because she whined and complained to her mother that Wayne was mean and called her names. This was the truth, because Wayne did not like her, and considered her a whiney brat.

By the time Wayne turned seven, his parents sold their home, located on the south side of the city and bought an apartment house on the north side of the city. Around the same time, Milton's parents sold their home and moved into a small home located on the east side of the city. Milton and Wayne continued to occasionally get together and play war games. Their new battleground was really 'cool' as it had places that could be used as bunkers and areas that were constantly on fire. Their new battlefield was located a short distance behind Wayne's house and happened to be the city dump. At the time preserving the environment was not a big concern and the Department of Environmental Conservation, had not been created, or, if it had, it was impotent and powerless, as the dump was located alongside a river and burnable trash burned virtually 24-hours each day.

Due to distance between residences, Gregory was no longer a playmate, and Wayne no longer had to contend with getting reprimanded for being mean to Gregory's little sister.

When Wayne was ten years old, his parents decided to escape city life, purchasing and moving into a small farm located several miles from the city. This move ended Milton and Wayne's ability to get together for play and the thing Wayne missed most about losing contact with Milton, was the fact Milton had the largest collection of comic books in the East. Both boys had spent many hours together engrossed in the episodes of "Dick Tracy," "Red Ryder," "Green Hornet," "The Phantom," "The Lone Ranger," and other comic book heroes.

The move required Wayne to enroll in a strange new school, in a small Village, located about 8 miles from the family farm. Wayne commenced riding a school bus, which was a total new experience for him. His first day of riding on the school bus proved quite traumatic; however, the details of that day will be featured in another story.

Wayne would enlist in the military while a senior in high school and the day after graduation he departed for military boot camp.

Milton continued attending school in the city where he was born and walked to school. He eventually graduated from the public high school in the city. His father, who worked in the city's maintenance department, managed to have his son hired as an assistant to the city's surveyor and Milton would eventually gain the position of County surveyor.

Around the same time that Wayne's parents purchased their farm, Gregory's parents also decided to abandon city life and purchased a small farm located a short distance outside the city. Gregory and his little sister commenced riding a school bus and attending school in a Village located just outside the city. Attending public school was a totally new experience for the two, because while living in the city, they attended a Catholic elementary school and walked to school. After graduating from high school, Gregory entered college, and worked at odd jobs. After attending college for a couple of years, he dropped out and joined the Navy.

Having completed a tour of duty in the United States Navy, Wayne returned home, and obtained employment in a local factory while waiting to be called to commence employment in the Federal Aviation Administration; a position he had applied for before being discharged. Now 21 years old, he purchased a new car and started looking for female companionship. His former steady girl friend, who had vowed to remain loyal and wait for him to return home from the military, was now married and had a child.

One afternoon, while driving down Main Street in the Village where he had graduated from school, Wayne saw three young women walking on the sidewalk and recognized them as former underclassmen. He stopped and asked the three if they would like a ride to their destination. All three, (having recognized him), got in the car and told Wayne to drop them at one of the girl's homes. Not wasting time, Wayne inquired as to whether any of the young women would be interested in going out on a date. Much to his chagrin, one informed him that she was engaged to be married and the other two advised that they had steady boyfriends. As they rode along, he learned that two of the girl's were in training to become Registered Nurses. One asked if he would be interested in going on a blind date with her roommate. Wayne immediately agreed, and it was decided the girl and her steady, would join Wayne and her roommate on a double date to see a movie. Date having been set, Wayne asked the name of his mystery date. Upon learning her name, he gulped and had reservations about whether the girl would want to go on a date when she learned the identity of the man she would be going out with. That girl was Gregory's little sister, whom Wayne had despised as a five year old. However, they had not seen each other in almost 18 years, and as it turned out, both were curious as to what the other would be like.

The blind date went very well. Wayne was delighted to find that the girl he had once despised had developed into an attractive young woman with a very enjoyable personality. Gregory's little sister was surprised and intrigued to find that the boy she once detested, had developed into a handsome young man with a charming personality. That first date led to another, and another, and within six months, Wayne asked

Gregory's little sister to become his wife. She immediately agreed and they decided to marry as soon as she graduated from nursing school. Throughout their long engagement, their love for each other grew stronger and stronger. As they did not have a great deal of money, their wedding was a rather simple affair concluding with a small reception of family and friends.

God works in mysterious ways and performs frequent miracles. Who would have guessed or even imagined that a boy and girl, who despised each other as children, would one day come together in love. Their love would produce five beautiful, intelligent, ambitious children; each of whom would become successful in adult life.

Milton, eventually married, and enjoyed a successful career working as a surveyor for the City of Cortland. Unfortunately, Milton passed away while in his sixties.

After discharge from the Navy, Gregory finished his college education. He found his niche in public education and became a school teacher. He married and the marriage produced two children. Gregory completed a long teaching career and retired to enjoy spending time boating and fishing. Unfortunately, he passed into eternal life in 2018.

Gregory's little sister Kathleen graduated from nursing school and worked several years as a Registered Nurse. After a stint as a substitute teacher of 2nd grade in Saint Peter's Elementary School, she was asked to accept a full time teaching position at the school. As she enjoyed teaching, she left her nursing career and completed 22 years teaching 2nd grade in two Catholic Elementary schools. Though enjoying her career, she proclaims that her favorite profession was being a "Mom."

At the time of this writing, Wayne (this author) and Gregory's 'little sister' Kathleen have been married 58 years and remain devoted to each other.

Life is full of challenges and uncertainties; however, God does work in mysterious ways and for whatever reason, He smiled upon me!

SHORTS THAT FIT WELL

WRECK-UM RALPH

It was a lovely spring morning and Marie opened her kitchen window to savor the fresh morning breeze. She stood at the window for a moment, studying a Ruby Throated Hummingbird that was hovering above a nectar feeder. While studying the colorful little bird, she said to herself, *Thank you God! You gave us so many beautiful things to enjoy.* As she started to turn from the window, her ears detected a faint, familiar sound, "meow." The sound seemed to be coming from beneath the Camellia bush just outside the window. "Meow," there it was again. The cry sounded weak and plaintive. *That sounds like a kitten in distress,* she thought. She went outside and found a small, grey and white kitten, estimated to be about 3 or 4 weeks old, huddled under her Camellia bush. Guessing that the kitten had either been abandoned or lost by its mother and was hungry, she returned to her kitchen, poured some milk onto a saucer and returned outside. She placed the saucer under the bush and the hungry little kitten immediately started lapping up the milk.

Marie studied the kitten as it consumed the milk and wondered where the little fur ball came from and how it found its way into her yard. Regardless, she couldn't abandon the poor little thing to an almost certain dire fate. There was an animal Veterinarian office located nearby and perhaps the workers there could find a home for the little fur ball. She managed to snatch up the kitten and although he struggled to get free, she maintained her hold on him. Returning to her kitchen, she retrieved her car keys and then placed the kitten in her car. Being trapped inside a vehicle caused the kitten to go into panic mode. He crawled under the car seat and huddled there shaking in fear of the unknown.

It was a short drive to the Vet's office and when she arrived, Marie retrieved the kitten from beneath the car seat and carried the frightened, meowing little guy into the office. She explained the kitten's plight to the receptionist in the office and was dismayed to learn that the office only treated animals. They did not recover, nor find homes for animals. The receptionist gave Marie directions to a, Friends of Animals facility, and Marie returned to her vehicle, nestling the frightened kitten in her arms. She got into her vehicle, placed the kitten on the seat beside her and started to pull out onto the highway. As she did, the kitten jumped off the seat and onto her legs. When this happened, she lost control of her vehicle and was struck by an oncoming vehicle. Marie and the other driver were injured; however, not seriously and the kitten jumped out of the car when someone opened the door. Having witnessed the accident, an employee in the Vet office, retrieved the frightened kitten carried it into the facility and placed it in a cage. The staff in the Vet's office immediately dubbed the kitten "Wreckum Ralph."

Wreckum Ralph was adopted into the Beyea home by a twist of fate. We were in the process of emotional healing from the sudden and unexpected death of Boots, when it happened. Boots had also found her way into our home by a twist of fate, or perhaps animal providence. Boots was a feral cat, living with her mother and identical two brothers, under our neighbor's tool shed. Her adoption into our family is another story.

Saddened by Boot's sudden demise, my wife was commiserating over our loss with our daughter, Nannette. Coincidentally, Nannette had just returned home from taking her dog to the vet. She related that while at the Vet's, she was asked if she knew anyone who would be interested in adopting a grey and white kitten, that was living in a cage at the Vet's office. She learned that animals without owners were turned over to the animal shelter, and that was about to become Ralph's fate. The office receptionist related the only reason Ralph was there was because of an unusual incident. She related the circumstances of Ralph's appearance and the accident the kitten had caused. It was explained that the kitten's origin was unknown and it may have problems because of becoming separated from its mother before being weaned.

Kathy listened to the story, saw the beautiful little frightened kitten, she was smitten and informed the receptionist that she would take the kitten into our home. The Veterinary informed Kathy that the kitten had been examined and given a rabies shot. A cardboard cat carrier was provided by the Vet, so that Ralph wouldn't cause another accident.

I was introduced to Ralph on his arrival at our home. Ralph greeted me with indifference and squirmed to escape when I tried to hold him.

We immediately fell in love with the little fur ball, and wanted to cuddle him.

As all cat owners know, cats, like people have their own unique personality. Alas, we quickly learned that Wreckum Ralph detests being held and he is definitely not a lap cat. Strangely, Ralph shows his affection by lying on our feet, or, our shoes. He has a real thing for shoes and we frequently find him snuggled up to them.

Ralph settled into our home and was enjoying the comfortable, leisure life of a spoiled pet. Then the unexpected happened. As previously mentioned, Boots was the female kitten in a set of triplets. We saw one of her brothers on a daily basis when I placed cat food outside. He was a tough, feral cat, who had survived outdoors for nearly two years, via cunning, agility, speed and strength. After placing food out in the afternoon, I sat on a glider nearby and watched the feral cat eat, while he eyed me suspiciously. One afternoon, as I sat on our glider, he brushed up against my leg and I reached down and petted him. That contact led to his gradually looking forward to the affection and eventually – like his sister – I won his affection. However, Blackie is another story and this story is about Ralph.

After adopting Ralph, we kept him inside, for fear of something happening to him if he went out. However, we began to feel sorry for

Ralph as he hung out at the door and continually begged to go outside. As our rear yard is entirely surrounded by fencing which includes shutting off our driveway, via a gate, we decided that if Ralph stayed in our back yard he would be safe. We closed the gate and let Ralph venture outside. His first outing could be described as tenuous. He hung out in the open door for a couple of minutes, sniffing the air apparently to detect any sign of danger. Then he slowly went outside, venturing no further than the line of Azalea bushes that surround our porch. What he discovered under the bushes is unknown. I imagined he was stalking bugs, or butterflies, or tracking the scent of a chipmunk. During the first two weeks of his adventures outside, he stayed close to the house. Then with every trip outside, he started branching out and began hunting chipmunks and birds. Apparently the 'Chippies' were too fast and elusive; however, unfortunately, he finally managed to catch a lovely little Finch. His attempts to catch butterflies that were attracted to our butterfly bushes, was hilarious as he leaped and jumped to no avail. Eventually, Ralph looked forward to his daily outings. We were pleased and happy that he confined his daily foray outside to our backyard and he made no attempt to go over, or under the fence.

As cat lovers, who have had various types and breeds of the 'fur balls', during our lives, Kathy and I recognized that virtually every cat we owned had a unique personality. Some were constantly seeking affection. Some loved to play with other cats – and in some cases – even dogs. Some were hunters, who enjoyed bringing us their trophy kill. (Snakes dropped at the door caused a shriek from Kathy). Others seemed to care less about hunting and lazed about knowing their 'Peep's' would feed them. As Ralph matured, we came to the conclusion that he was on the feline scale of autism. He absolutely refuses to sit or nestle on our lap. He dislikes being picked up and if we show him too much affection, such as scratching his neck or belly, he bites.

After observing that Ralph did not attempt to venture out of our yard, we felt that he was safe outside and would not encounter too much danger. Then, one afternoon, the unexpected happened. At the time, we were unaware that Blackie and Boots were part of a set of triplets. As usual Ralph was enjoying his outing and, thank goodness, I happened to be watching from our porch window. Suddenly, Boots and

Blackie's sibling appeared in the yard and immediately attacked Ralph. Poor Ralph had no concept of fighting for survival. He screamed and tried to run. I called to Kathy and we hurried outside. We could hear Ralph's plaintiff cries for help, coming from behind our garage, where the feral black cat had him pinned. As soon as we appeared the feral cat ran off. Poor Ralphie! He had a gaping wound on his back near his tail. I picked him up and he immediately calmed. Although his wound was not bleeding badly, we decided to take him immediately to the Vet.

Upon examining Ralph, the Vet told us it was a good thing we had brought Ralph for treatment, or the wound would probably have become infected. Ralph required surgery. After two days in the Vet hospital, we brought Ralph home. He was extremely uncomfortable because the Vet had attached an inverted V shaped collar on his neck, to prevent him from trying to get at and lick his wound. Ralph wobbled around our home for two weeks, aggravated by the nuisance on his neck and it was a challenge for him to eat. Thank goodness the wound healed quickly and the pesky collar was removed.

Subsequently, we decided that Ralph's forays outside were over and he would be confined to our home. Apparently, Ralph has forgotten the attack and he continues to lie by our back door, begging to go out into the big world. While lying on our enclosed glassed in porch, he eyes the outside world and as I study him, I wonder what he is thinking. I do know and appreciate his certain peculiarities; such as, jumping up onto the bathroom sink and begging to drink out of a dripping faucet. The need to be kissed on top of his head during this bathroom sink ritual and his sleeping on his back with his legs extended upward. Ralph has now lost the derogatory name of "Wreckum" and he is content, whenever he gets the chance to play 'pawsies' under a closed door, with Blackie. Will the two of them ever become "Best Buds"? Not! No way! But we love them both!

I conclude this story, by showing you Ralph, and you will understand why we love this grey fur ball.

"Hi! I love to show you my best side."

SHORTS THAT FIT WELL

THE MIRACLE OF BLACKIE

Having read this far in "Shorts That Fit Well" the reader is quite aware that cats and dogs have a special place in our hearts, and are very dear to us.

You have been treated to "Boots" and "Wreckum Ralph." Now it is Blackie's turn and the story of how he became a lover is truly a miracle.

Boot's sudden demise, caused us to adopt Ralph, the feral kitten. At the time, I was putting food out on a daily basis for a family of feral cats that lived under our neighbor's tool shed. I was particularly attracted to Boot's twin brother, who soon made it known, that he was a tough, agile, fearless little black panther. I watched in amazement as he leaped from the ground to the top of our seven foot fence, even clearing the fence when he wanted to. I often watched him climb to the top branches of the 60' Cherry tree in our back yard. He was also an amazing hunter. Blackie would lurk silently behind our Azalea bushes and suddenly, quick as a flash snatch an unsuspecting chipmunk. I even saw him leap and snatch birds out of the air. Studying the antics of the black fur-ball,

I became convinced it would not be possible to ever lay a hand on, or even touch, this handsome black and white cat.

I did enjoy watching the antics of the feral little panther and often sat on our outside glider watching him. Nearly two years passed and the black and white kitten developed into a muscular tom cat.

One evening, after having put out cat food, I was sitting on the glider focused on my cell phone. Suddenly, I felt a furry body brush up against my leg. Startled, I looked down and saw Blackie lying about two-feet away, staring at me. As a cat lover, I had read the book, "What My Cat Has Taught Me About Life." I stared at the cat, smiled and blinked my eyes. According to cat expert, Niki Anderson, "when a cat stares at you and blinks, he is telling you he loves you". The little Panther continued studying me and blinked his eyes several times. The following day, when I placed the food out, the little black-panther brushed against my leg and I managed to pet him. By the end of that week, I was able to pick the black-panther up and pet him. I immediately dubbed him, "Blackie." He obviously enjoyed my petting him as we continued our daily love sessions. However, Blackie continued to live under our neighbor's tool shed.

One afternoon, I called Kathy outside, while Blackie was rubbing against me and invited her to pet him. When she did, Blackie bit her hand, causing a puncture wound. Kathy cried out and Blackie fled to the safe haven of his shed. Kathy washed the bite but, as the bite was from a feral cat we were concerned about infection; or worse, the possibility of rabies. I took Kathy to the hospital emergency room, where they cleaned the bite and gave her medication. We were informed by hospital personnel that all bite wounds caused by wild animals had to be reported to County Animal Control. Hospital personnel had already contacted Animal Control and we waited for their arrival in the hospital. A young man and young woman - both very polite – appeared at the hospital, and after learning the source of the bite, informed us that they would have to trap the feral cat that caused the bite, to have it tested and given a rabies shot. Leary as to what the cat's fate would be after being captured, we were told the cat would also be neutered, and turned over to Friends of Animals, for possible adoption. I asked the officers if they would please return the cat to our property after performing the work. They said they would.

That evening, the Animal Control officers placed a 'catch cage' containing tempting morsels of cat food in our driveway. Actually, as we would later learn, it probably was not necessary to bait the trap, because Blackie is a very curious cat and feels the need to explore every strange place.

After just two nights, the little black-panther was caught, and I moped around for three days worrying about his fate. On the morning of the 4th day, I went outside and surprise, there was Blackie sitting in our driveway. However, at first I wasn't sure it was him. He appeared to have been in a fight, as half of one ear had been bitten off. I called Animal Control to ask what happened and was informed that it was their policy to snip off half of an animal's ear so as to be able to identify that the animal had already received their rabies shot, if necessary to capture it again.

Blackie was pleased to be back and immediately decided he needed to prove his affection by rubbing against me and letting me pet him. That day we decided to introduce Blackie to our home, and to Ralph. Blackie explored his new digs, curious about everything, then jumped in my lap and gave me a purr of approval. At first, Blackie treated Ralph with indifference, and Ralph eyed the black intruder with disdain. Ralph had been neutered as a kitten, whereas, Blackie as an adult tomcat, who possibly may have fathered kittens. Though neutered, Blackie proved he was determined to be the Alfa male and was taking charge. Ralph and Blackie's inability to get along presented a challenge. We loved them both and decided to keep them separated.

As Blackie had lived outside for nearly two years and was a proven tough guy, we continued to let him outside when he asked to go out. We were pleased that at the end of each day, he reappeared and asked to come in. We knew Blackie could handle the challenges outside well, and didn't worry about him. Then, one afternoon at meal time, no Blackie! As daylight turned to darkness, he had not appeared and we began to worry. Perhaps a person who did not like cats had done something to him. He did not appear that night, nor did he appear the next day. We fretted and worried imagining all sort of horrible things. The days turned into weeks, and with heavy hearts, we accepted that our black, loving fur-ball had met his demise. Three weeks passed. Suddenly, one morning at the start of the 4th week, I heard Kathy calling to me, "Wayne, Blackie is in the kitchen window!" I quickly responded, and yes, there he was! It was our beloved Blackie, albeit, gaunt in appearance and meowing frantically. I opened the door and he came bounding in. He immediately headed for Ralph's food dish and gobbled down food. Then he lapped water for several minutes. After sating his hunger and thirst, he rubbed against both Kathy and I, meowing in either a greeting, or attempt to tell us the trauma he had endured.

I came to the conclusion that curious cat that he was, he somehow went inside something; perhaps an open tool shed, and got closed inside. I shudder to think of his hunger, thirst and panic, as the days passed while being trapped.

Perhaps our prayers for our Blackie reached the proper venue, and he escaped before starving or dying of thirst. After that scary episode, we decided that both Ralph and Blackie would be confined to our home.

Strangely, Blackie's near death experience caused him to lose desire for the outdoors. He stopped asking to go out and apparently has no desire to go outside.

The once strong, fearless, feral, lithe small black- panther, has settled into the good life of a house cat. Every day, he follows me about the house and when I am on my computer he snuggles up on the desktop beside me. When I go outside our home, or leave on some errand, he seeks Kathy out and sleeps in her lap.

How I wish Blackie was able to share his adventures with us. However, the fact that he provides Kathy and I so much love and joy is all that matters.

"Now, how am I going to capture that bird?"

SHORTS
THAT
FIT WELL

THE SAINT WHO
WORE A BOLO TIE

This is the story of "Saint Bob," who earned sainthood via performing extraordinary acts of kindness, charity, compassion and devotion to his faith.

As a practicing Catholic, I have always been interested in learning about Saints, particularly as to how they achieved Sainthood.

Those who have studied and shown interest in the lives of saints know that achieving sainthood is a difficult task. Acquiring Sainthood requires spiritual and Godly behavior far above the norm. To achieve Sainthood, a mortal must please God, by demonstrating kindness and compassion beyond the range of normal human behavior and not fear sacrificing one's self in the process. For most Catholics, the Sisters of Loreto Nun, Mother Teresa comes to mind.

I must admit that a "Saint I ain't," and throughout most of my life, I never imagined that I would be privileged to meet or know a person destined for sainthood. Now, I consider myself fortunate for being permitted to befriend a man who during his life on earth, was on the path to sainthood. Sadly, I did not recognize that fact until God called him home.

I first met "Bob" when I started participating in our church's "Feed the Homeless program." Bob actively participated in the program and his service went beyond the pale of just feeding the homeless. Bob, worked at motivating those that we were feeding to become active, contributing members of society. He spent time and resources working one-on-one, with those experiencing alcohol, drug or mental problems and perhaps in despair, toward putting them on a road to recovery.

Unfortunately, I did not get to know "Bob" until he was in his late 70's and I was immediately attracted to his warm smile, his deep voice, his warm personality, his quick wit and his laughter. I learned that "Bob" was the father of 9 children, loved his wife dearly and that she had recently passed away.

Bob was a man of average height and build. There was nothing physically imposing about him and his most obvious strengths seemed to be his warm personality, his honesty, his sincerity. He portrayed the sense of being a kind and gracious man, having no interest in offending or hurting anyone.

Upon learning that "Bob" had earned his living as an accountant, I was curious as to how having money and material possessions seemed the least important factor in his life.

Having diminished hearing, I always looked forward to having "Bob" lector at Mass, because his deep bass voice was easy to hear and he had the ability to bring the scriptural reading to life.

Though residing in Georgia, "Bob" was completely smitten, and bitten, by everything connected with the western United States. He loved horses! He made numerous trips out west, where he rode horses and imagined he was a cowboy. Bob portrayed his love for the west by always wearing a 'bolo' string tie, rather than a necktie, whether lecturing at church, or attending a formal function.

Bob was loved and appreciated by all who knew him; however, it was not just his personality that determined sainthood. A sense of humor was one of his fortes and he loved making people laugh. When out to eat with our group from church, he always ordered a dessert with his meal and when it was delivered, he would put his arms around it and proclaim. "This is all mine and you aren't getting any of it." That proclamation always inspired laughter, which was his intended goal. The reality was, if anyone had asked him to share the dish, he would have handed the dessert to them.

I would learn that "Bob" continually sought ways that he could help mankind. At 80 years of age, "Bob" became a volunteer at a local hospital. His unpaid duties involved assisting the elderly and handicapped to access and exit the hospital. I also learned that Bob's children had been giving him new clothes as birthday and Christmas presents, and they asked why they never saw him wearing them. He responded that he no longer had the clothes as he gave them to the homeless.

However, his work at the hospital and charitable gift giving wasn't enough. He felt that God was calling him to perform a special service, a service that most men; especially of his age, would have been reluctant to perform. Many would probably even deem what "Bob" was about to undertake repugnant.

Bob discovered a small, frail, disabled (missing one leg), middle-aged woman, in all likelihood an alcoholic who spent every day seated in a wheel chair upon the exit ramp of one of Atlanta's busiest highways. The woman held a sign in her lap which stated she was disabled and in need of money. In all likelihood, motorists who observed the pitiful little beggar experienced various emotions. Some felt sorry for her and handed her money. Some stared straight ahead and tried their best to ignore her. Others, and hopefully they were few, rudely yelled obscenities at her.

I must admit that I observed the pitiful sight on several occasions and even learned her name; however, I convinced myself she was just another one of society's losers, bumming money for alcohol, rather than seeking rehabilitation while living in a shelter and I ignored her plight.

The dirty little beggar in the wheel chair, became a topic of conversation with friends and I was told the woman was an alcoholic, having lost a leg via some unknown cause; that she turned down residency in a shelter and at night slept under a highway overpass.

I was unaware that "Bob" had taken on the mission of helping and rehabilitating the woman, until a mutual female friend of Bob and I, told me that she had been asked by "Bob" to scrub the woman in a shower, if he brought the woman to her. Bob explained that he had discovered the woman needed dental work and when he took her to his dentist, he refused to work on her teeth because she smelled so bad. My friend told me that she was reluctant to bring the derelict woman into her home and wondered where it would be possible and appropriate to give the woman a shower. I was shocked to learn Bob was committed to helping the little beggar and suggested bathing her in a shower at one of the truck stops located at several exits of the Atlanta beltway. I also suggested that if she did this, she obtain the assistance of another woman.

Upon learning the information about giving the derelict a shower, I confronted Bob, and asked him how involved he had become with assisting the derelict. Of course, as expected, he responded displaying his charming smile as he told me that he was quite committed to doing all that he could for the woman.

I praised him for taking on what appeared to be an insurmountable task, but cautioned that he should not under any circumstances, bring the woman to his home and be alone with her. My always suspicious police mind caused me to warn him that if he brought her into his home, she might steal something, or would try to extort money from him by making some false claim. I was shocked to learn Bob had already commenced bringing her to his home, where he fed her and gave her money. Bob told me he was personally touched by the woman's plight and was determined to do his best to get her off the booze and get her functioning in society.

Eventually, Bob brought the woman to a local truck stop, where two lady friends were waiting. They assisted the woman into a shower stall and scrubbed her with strong soap, using brushes. When she came out of the shower – so I was told – Bob had new clothes for her to put on. Then he took her back to his dentist, who performed the work on the woman's teeth. It is reasonable to presume that Bob paid whatever the amount was for the dental work. Where Bob took her after the dental visit is unknown to me; however, I believe he either took her to his home, or, Must Ministries, a well-known center for aiding the homeless.

Most of Bob's friends were now aware of his dedication toward redeeming the little exit ramp beggar; however, when the subject was broached with Bob, he just smiled and responded that all was going as well as could be expected.

During one of our conversations, I informed Bob that from my perspective, it was highly unlikely the woman, whom I shall refer to as Clara, could be salvaged. I told him to be on his guard and it would be wise not to be alone with her.

Bob listened; however, a voice much more powerful than mine was guiding him. He just smiled, thanked me for my concern and replied that though having alcohol and mental problems, the woman presented no threat.

It was previously pointed out that Bob possessed a warm personality and was well liked by everyone who knew him. His smile and sincere, deep laughter, made those around him feel relaxed and at peace.

One evening, Bob was invited to a friend's home for dinner and conversation. While relaxing after dinner and, while laughing heartily, Bob was suddenly summoned by God. He slumped in his chair, stopped breathing and he was gone! Those with him at the time, later told me that he passed from life while laughing and apparently without pain. He was 80 years old when he passed and his mind remained sharp to the end.

Bob's funeral was well attended, as there were many who knew and loved him. Sadly, I was in New York at the time and was unable to attend the final tribute to my friend. I would later learn that his children and their children nearly filled the center section of the church. I also learned that so many people attended the funeral it was necessary to assign a traffic director for vehicles entering the church parking lot. A passing motorist, delayed behind the line of vehicles waiting to enter the church parking areas, asked the traffic director, "What happened? Did a Priest die?"

The traffic director replied, "No Sir, not a Priest, just a very good man." A succinct, heartfelt tribute to a man who during his time on earth, brought joy to many people.

I did not inquire as to whether the derelict little beggar woman attended Bob's funeral, and with my always suspicious police mind, assumed she was probably back on the highway exit ramp soliciting money.

I was wrong! I would later learn that Bob had succeeded in rehabilitating the woman. She had given up drinking and was living with relatives, whom had been located either by Bob, or someone he had solicited for help.

I am now convinced that Bob achieved Sainthood and he is at peace in Heaven. Only a Saint could master the awesome challenge of recovering a seemingly, totally lost soul.

God Bless you Bob and I hope to one day see you and hear your hearty laughter. It will be interesting to see if God permits you to wear a "Bolo" tie in Heaven.

Saint Bob

IT'S A GAME ONLY FOR RICH PEOPLE

"That is a game played only by rich people," was my father's response as he drove by our local country club, with me seated beside him. I was perhaps ten years old at the time and was fascinated by the luxurious looking premises, having what appeared to be perfectly manicured, verdant lawns. As we passed the long driveway leading to what appeared to be an elegant large home, I saw four men standing in a spot, each, holding what appeared to be a club. Curious as to what the place was and what the men were doing, I asked, "Pa, what is that place and what are those men doing?"

He responded, "That is the Cortland Country Club. They are playing the game of golf."

"Have you ever played golf?" I asked.

"Nope, it costs a lot of money. Golf is a game played only by rich people and we aren't rich."

The years passed by. Although gainfully employed and earning a comfortable income (most of the time), I was not becoming rich, did not play golf and turned down offers to play the game.

At age 49, having completed 25 years in the New York State Police, I was offered a job in Security for a large utility company. It was a lucrative offer, so I reluctantly retired from a career that I loved and accepted my new employment.

My workmates in the State Police feted me at a retirement dinner, during which I was both praised and roasted. At the conclusion of the fun-filled affair, I was presented with a set of golf clubs. I presumed the clubs were given as encouragement to take up the game, or, as a joke gift.

Having never played golf, I placed the golf clubs in my garage and considered selling them.

On my first day of work in my new employment, I was engaged in settling my office, when my manager suddenly appeared. He (Don), handed me a cup ot coffee and asked, "What are your plans for the day?"

I thanked Don for the coffee and responded, "You're the boss, what do you want me to do?"

Displaying a smile, he responded, "Do you have your tools with you?"

Puzzled at what tools I was supposed to have brought to my employment, I answered, "What tools am I supposed to have?"

The man who was my immediate boss, and a man, whom I would eventually come to admire and love responded – displaying an impish grin – "Golf clubs! Our management team plays a lot of golf."

This unexpected response caused me to laugh. I responded, "I must advise you that I have never played the game of golf; however, probably as a joke gift, I was presented with a set of golf clubs when I retired."

"Good!" He replied, "Go home and get them. We have a 10:30 tee time."

How strange it seemed, that on my first day of work in my new career, I found myself on a golf course, playing a game I had never played before.

I rode with Don to the golf course, where he introduced me to Company Vice Presidents Carl and John.

Upon returning home to pick up my golf clubs, I changed from suit and tie into casual slacks and a golf shirt, so I was appropriately attired for my first adventure onto a golf course.

After being introduced to my golf partners, and before teeing off, I felt the need to inform them I had never played golf and did not know much about the game.

Don, Carl and John were gracious and advised that as no money was being wagered, they would be happy to teach me the game.

As I recall, my score that day was 120; however, I found the game to be enjoyable and knew I would improve.

Although my playing partners were avid players, I discovered none of them would ever compete professionally, as all three of them, normally scored in the 90's.

We concluded the day by sharing drinks and eating dinner in a local restaurant. All in all, my first day of employment in my new career, set the tone for an anticipated joy-filled career. I discovered that our management group played golf often, and my game steadily improved. However, I was never interested in taking lessons from a professional golf instructor and it was obvious I would never become a scratch golfer.

After passage of a couple of months, my manager started advising me of the dates our company executives planned to appear, and I became responsible for scheduling our tee times.

A few years passed, Don, who was a 40-year employee with the company, retired and was replaced by another long time employee, promoted from the union force to management. The new manager did not play golf, nor was he interested in developing a relationship outside work. I requested a transfer to our Company's northernmost district, with office located in Plattsburgh, New York.

I had visited this district before to assist my security counterpart, and fell in love with beautiful Lake Champlain. When the Security Investigator in Plattsburgh suddenly resigned and moved to Florida, I immediately requested to fill that position. My request was granted and the company even paid my moving expenses.

Kathy and I purchased a lovely small, wood frame home at lakeside, in Cliff Haven, located just south of Plattsburgh. Cliff Haven was directly across Route 9W from Plattsburgh Air Force Base, which was decommissioned by our government in 1995. We would discover that the vast majority of home owners in Cliff Haven were U.S. Air Force retirees.

Shortly after moving to Cliff Haven, I joined a local golf club. As a member of a golf club, my play steadily improved despite the fact I had not taken up the game until age 49, and had never taken a golf lesson.

The final year of my membership in the golf club on Lake Champlain; on the season's final day, which concluded with a banquet and awarding of prizes, I surprised myself by playing my best game ever. I won three prizes; longest drive, closest to the pin (10 inches) and low score with handicap.

The following spring of the year, we moved to Georgia, and I immediately joined a local golf club. After getting acclimated at my new golf course, I hooked up with regular playing partners and we became the best of friends. Our wives also became friends, and I suggested that once each year, we should travel and play golf in another state. The deal was, the men would play golf and our wives would sight see or shop. It was agreed and I volunteered to make reservations for our first golf outing. I naturally thought of Lake Champlain and knew that my playing partners would enjoy Bluff Point Golf Course, located on the shore of the lake. Rental cabins located in the center of the course were reserved for the week of July 4th. I also agreed to drive up to Bluff Point and take everyone's golf equipment. The rest of our group flew into Burlington, Vt. and rented a vehicle. It turned out to be a very enjoyable time for everyone.

A member of our foursome, happened to own property in Boseman, Montana, and it was decided the following July, we would vacation and play golf in Montana. Once again, Kathy and I drove, carrying the golf equipment, while the remainder of our group flew into Helena, then rented a vehicle and drove to Bozeman. The drive to Montana was very enjoyable. On the way, we visited St. Louis, Mount Rushmore, the Badlands, Black Hills Park, the Custer State Park, Little-Big Horn, a former gold mine, a ghost town and spent three days in Yellowstone Park on our return trip home. We will never forget the drive out of the north entrance of Yellowstone Park, on the 6th of July. We were at 11,400 foot elevation and driving in a raging snow storm.

On our drive home, we side-trekked to Forest Lake, Minnesota and visited Wayne's eldest sister, Norma. As I had not seen Norma in several years, it proved to be a happy, emotional visit.

That combination golf/tourist vacation was very enjoyable and we started planning our next adventure.

The following year reservations were made at a resort in Hilton Head, South Carolina, where we could play three separate golf courses. Another very enjoyable summer vacation and proved so enjoyable, we returned there the following year.

Somehow, I became an avid golfer and find it a game that is fun and relaxing.

Now, in my old age I continue to belong to a golf club, although I do not play as often as I used to and my game is not as sharp as it once was, but it is still enjoyable.

My father's answer to my question all those years ago; "That is a game played only by rich people," now inspires a chuckle. I certainly am not rich monetarily; however, I consider myself rich in friendship with fellow golfers and wonderful spiritual people.

I want to say, "Dad, golf is not a game just for rich people. Golf provides the means to bring people together in friendship and joy. It saddens me to realize that my workaholic father, who routinely labored seven days each week, never tried to play the game he considered only rich people played. I believe he would have enjoyed the game and the camaraderie of relaxation with friends.

SHORTS THAT FIT WELL

HAV - N - FUN

After becoming entrenched in my second career and viewing the majesty and beauty of Lake Champlain, I asked to transfer to Plattsburgh, New York, when our company's northernmost division needed a replacement in the Security Department. My request was not motivated by seeking a better work environment. My motivation was the lure of beautiful Lake Champlain, and plan to purchase a home on the lake.

I became attracted to Lake Champlain, while assisting my security department counterpart in the Plattsburgh office conduct a special investigation. When he announced that he was leaving employment and moving to the State of Florida, I volunteered to transfer to Plattsburgh. My offer was quickly accepted and I was pleased when the company agreed to pay my moving expenses. At the time, Kathy was a teacher at Saint Peter's School in Liberty, New York, and decided she could not move until the end of the school year. We put our home in Liberty, New York up for sale, and our 15-year old daughter, Kelly went to Plattsburgh with Dad. I rented a suite of rooms in a Plattsburgh motel, enrolled Kelly at Seton Catholic High in Plattsburgh, and started search for a lakeside home. As if in answer to my prayers, I happened upon a lovely, wood frame home, located at lakeside in the community of Cliff Haven. Cliff Haven is a residential community located on the south side of the city, adjacent to Plattsburgh Air Force Base, which the government decommissioned and ceased using as a military base in 1995. Upon viewing the small, but warm and inviting home on the west shore of Lake Champlain, my wife was pleased. Having moved ten times during our marriage because of transfers by my employer, we looked forward to leading a happy life of retirement on – what we would soon come to refer to as – 'our lake.'

We settled into our small, but lovely dream home and spent many hours on our home's 40' x 14' deck enjoying a vista that could be described as a living canvas of beautiful scenic splendor. The Green Mountains of Vermont stood as sentinels to the east. The Adirondack Mountains of New York stood as sentinels to the west. We enjoyed studying historic Crab Island, located about a mile off shore, with binoculars. I had learned that during the War of 1812, a small American Navy, anchored in Plattsburgh Bay, (visible to the north) under the command of a young Commodore by the name of Thomas Macdonough, fought and defeated the mighty British Navy. We learned that during the engagement, Crab Island was designated as a hospital for treatment of the wounded and dying from both sides of the conflict. It was reported that 150 British and Americans who died during the engagement were buried alongside each other on the island. In the early 1900's an obelisk was erected on the island to commemorate the historic battle and honor those who died. The northern end of historic Valcour Island was visible to the south and the channel between the west shore of Lake Champlain and the island was historic for providing haven to a small flotilla of American Revolutionary sailors, under the command of Benedict Arnold, who under the cover of dense fog, hid from the British Navy in the channel.

We watched magnificent Bald Eagles, swoop like dive bombers and snatch fish from the lake.

For over a year, we were content to relax on our deck and enjoy the beauty created by God. However, something was missing. Lovely sailboats silently glided on the lake's surface and motor boats of varying size, description and power, skipped along, leaving a rolling wake behind them. We longed for adventure and wanted to explore 'our' magnificent lake. One morning, while reading our company bulletin board, a "For Sale" notice caught my eye. Our Division Maintenance Supervisor posted that he was selling his 19' Magnum, inboard motor boat, with boat trailer. The notice stated the boat was 5 years old, but in excellent condition.

I immediately expressed an interest and travelled to my co-workers home to examine the boat, which sat affixed to a boat trailer in his yard. The boat appeared to be in excellent condition and I immediately made him an offer, which he accepted. Having purchased the boat, I had to make the decision as to where it would be berthed. We did not have a dock at our residence so it would be necessary to either rent a slip in the Valcour Marina, or, keep the boat on its trailer, parked in our driveway. However, there was an alternative. Our home was located just four houses from the Cliff Haven cove, and many home owners kept their boats on a mooring buoy in the cove. I purchased a mooring buoy, and placed it in the cove, within sight of our home. Having the boat moored in the lake would provide easier access than pulling it to a boat launch; launching it and reloading it on the trailer, every time we went out onto the lake. The mooring buoy worked fine and when it was moored we could keep watch on it from our home.

A new adventure was about to begin, because, despite having served in the United States Navy, I had never owned or operated a boat. I was eager and excited to become a boat Captain. Now I needed to learn every detail about operating our lovely inboard boat with carpeted deck, modified cabin and powered by a 276 hp, Chevrolet engine. I learned that the boat could cruise at 30 mph on a calm lake surface.

After our mooring buoy was in place, I was ready to launch our boat and felt a sense of relief when the previous owner said he would accompany me on my maiden launch. He would show me how to launch the boat from its trailer and help me attach the boat to my mooring buoy. The afternoon we launched he asked what sort of 'dingy' I had fastened to the mooring buoy, for our return to shore after the boat was attached to the buoy. He did not seem pleased, when I told him a canoe. We had purchased a sleek canoe shortly after moving into our new home and having mastered operation of the canoe, I thought it would serve as a fine means of travelling from shore to boat and boat to shore.

I was pleased when our launch of the boat from the Peru public boat launch site went well. I was equally pleased when I quickly took control of the boat's operation, while proudly wearing my new Captain's hat with gold braid on the brim. Though nervous, I managed to easily maneuver the boat up to its mooring buoy, and we tied up. Then things started going awry. Apparently, the former boat owner, teaching me the operation of a 276 hp boat, was not familiar with canoe nomenclature. He was a man of heavy build and he stepped from the boat ladder into the canoe before I grasped the canoe to steady it.

The canoe immediately rolled over and he dropped into the lake, managing to keep his hold on the boat ladder as the canoe rolled. I helped him clamber back aboard the boat. Then I went down the boat ladder, righted the canoe, which was now half full of water and pulled it against the boat. Though having little to no experience operating power boats, I was an excellent swimmer, lifeguard and water safety instructor. I held the canoe against the boat and helped my embarrassed mentor and companion get seated in the canoe. After he was seated, I suggested he sit very still. Then I got into the canoe and paddled us into shore. My mentor thanked me, turned down an offer to come inside our home to dry out and relax and hurriedly departed.

The following day at work, I learned that he had broken two ribs when the canoe overturned and his body slammed against the steps of the boat ladder.

Now that we had a boat, Kathy and I were eager to set forth on 'our lake' to explore and seek adventure. We were unaware that as it would turn out, we would experience many adventures. Some were pleasurable and others were downright scary; however, first things first. We needed a name for our little cruiser. I cannot recall how many names we considered before finally coming to the conclusion that having purchased the boat for fun and adventure, the appropriate name would be, "Hav-n-Fun." Within short order, I affixed letter decals to the stern and we christened 'Hav-n-Fun' by drinking a wine toast on board.

Our first outing on 'our lake,' proved to be our first scary adventure. Not being familiar with the process of tying our canoe to our mooring and disconnecting 'Hav-n-Fun' from the mooring, we tied the canoe to 'Hav-n-Fun,' then clambered on board. I started the engine, left the transmission in neutral and then returned to the canoe. I unfastened 'Hav-n-Fun' from the mooring and was in the process of tying the canoe to the mooring, when I noticed 'Hav-n-Fun,' with Kathy on board was drifting away. Waves rolling in from the lake were pushing 'Hav-n-Fun' toward the Rocks at the point of our cove. I yelled at Kathy to put the boat in gear and steer away from the rocks.

She called back, "How do I do that?"

Oh-oh, I quickly untied the canoe and paddled desperately to reach our boat. About ten feet from 'Hav-n-Fun' I dove into 'our lake,' and quickly swam to the boat ladder. I clambered aboard 'Hav-n-Fun' when it was only about one more wave movement from contacting the sharp rocks. I put the boat in gear and backed away from the rocks, then, we retrieved our canoe and towed it back to our mooring.

Upon conclusion of this embarrassing start of our first outing on 'Hav-n-Fun,' we enjoyed cruising smoothly on 'our lake' and went down to Westport and back. This was the farthest we had ventured on 'our lake' and as yet, I was not an experienced boat captain. As we approached the marina at Westport, I noticed 'Hav-n-Fun' needed fuel. I cruised slowly past the dock looking for a slip to tie up in. On my second pass, the dock-master signaled me to tie up in a small space between a large sailboat and a three deck cruiser. I gulped and told Kathy to get ready to grab onto a dock pylon to tie up. I jockeyed 'Hav-n-Fun' into the space and Kathy reached for the pylon. Stupidly, I still had our boat in gear and she was nearly pulled out of the boat before I stopped. She screamed at me to stop and I did. We tied up and I breathed a sigh of relief for not hitting the sailboat or cruiser. As we clambered onto the dock, we saw people sitting on the cruiser staring at us. They had obviously watched our horrible first docking and I felt embarrassed. I tried to ignore the stares and told myself, *oh well, we provided entertainment for them.* All in all, the day went well and when we returned to our mooring that evening, I decided to tie 'Hav-n-Fun' to the moor via bow cleats instead of the hook on the front of the bow.

Kathy and I would have many happy and many scary adventures cruising Lake Champlain on 'Hav-n-Fun.' One afternoon, we cruised across the lake to the East side of Grand Isle and visited what would become one of our favorite marina cafes in Vermont. It was a lovely afternoon, and the lake was calm. When we returned to 'Hav-n-Fun' for the return trip home; shortly after starting the engine, I smelled gas. However, the engine seemed to be running fine, so I decided to wait until we returned to our mooring to check out the problem. We cruised home and after attaching to the mooring, I opened the engine compartment. I turned white, gulped, looked upward and said aloud, "Thank You God!" The line that fed gas to the carburetor had split and gas was squirting onto the hot engine. Why the boat did not explode into fire and possibly kill us both, was a miracle. The next day I had 'Hav-n-Fun' towed down to Valcour Marina where a new gas line was installed.

One lovely Sunday, we decided to travel north on the lake into Canada. I was surprised to learn there was no requirement to stop at a border check point. The lake surface was like glass and we cruised at around 20 mph for most of the trip. We stopped at the Marina in Rouses Point, to enjoy a meal then headed home. As we neared Chazy, I noticed we were low on fuel. I cruised into the Chazy Marina to purchase gas. Oh oh! There was a sign which stated the Marina's gas facility was closed on Sundays. We returned to the lake and headed south. About a half mile north of the Cumberland Head/Grand Isle ferry crossing, we ran out of gas. Fortunately, 'Hav-n-Fun' was equipped with a marine radio. I radioed the Coast Guard station, located in Burlington, Vermont, and advised them of our situation. The dispatcher responded that he would notify a Vermont State Police boat patrol to respond as they carried emergency fuel. About a half hour later, two young Vermont Troopers appeared and gave me two gallons of free gas. I thanked them and they went on their way. After starting the engine we continued south toward home. As we approached Plattsburgh Bay, I considered cruising into the Marina to purchase fuel; however, I decided as the bay was very large, going into the Marina would be just as far as going to our moor in Cliff Haven. As it turned out this was a bad decision. We ran out of fuel again about one-half mile from our mooring. I was too embarrassed to call on our radio for help again. Kathy asked if I intended to attach a line to my body and swim towing the boat. I knew that was not possible and pondered our situation. Then we noticed a young fellow skimming nearby on a jet ski. I blew our boat horn to get his attention and he pulled up alongside. When I explained our situation, we tied a line to his jet ski and he towed us into our moor. We learned that the lad was the son of one of our neighbor's and he refused the payment I offered him.

One of my most embarrassing lake experiences occurred one Sunday afternoon, after inviting guests to join us on a lake cruise. The wives of our guests were teachers at the same school, where Kathy taught and I knew both of their husbands. We invited them to our home for a barbecue dinner and boat ride. When preparing to go out on the lake, I explained that it would be a challenge for the women to board our boat from a canoe. I suggested Kathy escort our guests down to the Cliff Haven cove beach and I would pick them up. The women agreed; however, their husbands opted to ride out to 'Hav-n-Fun' in the canoe with me. The short canoe ride out to our mooring went smoothly and I held the canoe firmly against 'Hav-n-Fun' while both men climbed aboard. We were engaged in conversation as I commenced disconnecting 'Hav-n-Fun' from its mooring. I was seated in the canoe and started to tie it to the moor, when suddenly, a heavy swell, created by a passing boat, rocked 'Hav-n-Fun.' The bow of the boat came down on the canoe dumping me in the lake. I was fully dressed at the time, with my wallet in my pants pocket. Now in the water, I called up to my passengers, "Larry, you will find a boat hook in the portside compartment."

Larry replied, "Okay, I found it. What am I supposed to do with it?"

Neither of the men had seen me dump into the lake and were unaware I was in the water. As calmly as possible, I replied, "Hook the canoe and hold it against the boat."

Larry carried out my instructions and both men were surprised when their totally soaked boat Captain climbed up the aft ladder and came on board. As I stood on deck with water dripping from my body, I was very embarrassed. However, we shared a laugh and then cruised into our cove where the woman boarded. I explained what happened and we shared group laughter. Then we cruised around Valcour and

Crab Islands. All in all, it proved to be a fun afternoon, and I provided our guests a humorous story to share with friends.

As a novice sailor, I soon came to the conclusion I needed to take a boating nomenclature and navigation certification course and learned the Coast Guard provided this training free. I convinced Kathy to attend the course with me and our friends Leo and Eileen Ward, also novice sailors, joined us. We attended the required training sessions at Clinton County Community College, and the instructor was excellent. There was an written examination upon conclusion of the training and I surprised myself by scoring 100 on the exam. Kathy passed with flying colors also and we were now card carrying certified marine navigation experts.

One summer afternoon on arrival home from work, I noticed the lake was very calm and suggested to Kathy that we go out on the lake and eat dinner onboard 'Hav-n-Fun.' She prepared a basket of food and we went out on our boat. As previously mentioned, the lake was like glass. I pushed the throttle forward and we glided out on the lake at about 30 mph. After skimming along for about a mile, our attention was drawn to a concentrated area of turmoil and waves. As we rapidly approached the area, we observed what appeared to be the dragon like head of some sort of creature. Whatever the creature was, it was obviously large and created waves as it swam. As we drew near, the waves created by whatever was in the water, caused 'Hav-n-Fun' to rock and roll. Suddenly the creature dove and within a minute the lake surface was like glass again. We wondered what we had just witnessed and wondered if we had just seen 'Champ' the supposedly mythical lake monster. We cruised into a cove on the east side of Valcour Island, anchored and ate our dinner. While dining, we conversed about the 'thing' we saw in 'our lake.'

My friend Frank Pabst, Captain of the Lake Champlain cruise boat Juniper, scoffed at reported sightings of Champ and told me that what folks were seeing was just an "anomaly in the lake." However, Kathy and I agreed we saw some sort of creature that resembled an alligator, crocodile, or dragon, and we had not had any alcoholic beverages prior to our seeing it. This sighting inspired me to include 'Champ' in my novel, "The Treasure of Valcour Island." Will also mention that Captain

Frank Pabst was such an interesting and unusual man, I sought his permission to pen his life story. The Captain consented and was elated that he would be memorialized.

Captain Frank was a prolific and interesting story teller, though writing his biography proved challenging as he skipped from one story to the next, leaving gaps in between. We spent many hours together and all in all, the undertaking was an enjoyable experience resulting in, "The Captain of the Juniper."

While exploring 'our lake' we discovered Otter Creek, a wide stream that flowed into Lake Champlain, on the Vermont side of the lake. Otter Creek is navigable for 8 miles from the lake up to lovely water falls in Vergennes, Vermont. We boated up the creek to Vergennes on several occasions and enjoyed seeing Otter (hence the stream's name) playing at creek side and hundreds of Osprey nested along the banks of the Creek.

One of our most memorable and enjoyable lake outings occurred on a lovely Sunday, summer afternoon, when we decided to explore the east side of Grand Isle and travel north into Canada. It was the first time we toured the East side of 'our lake' all the way to Missisquoi Bay in Quebec, Canada. Sighting a marina in the bay, we docked to obtain fuel and explore the shoreline. Another boat, a little larger than ours, tied up beside us at the marina's dock. The Dock Master, proved to be French Canadian and it soon appeared he intended to fleece the two boat captains from the United States. He spoke to us in French and pretended (quite obvious he was lying) that he did not understand much English and could not speak it. Although he was able to clearly state in English, "Cash only."

Fortunately, the Captain of the other boat and I, had enough cash with us to pay for fuel. The man and wife in the other boat had two very handsome and friendly Irish Setter dogs with them on their boat, and as we fueled I complemented him on his boat and dogs. The very warm and friendly couple introduced themselves as Dave and Margo Marvin, residents of Vermont, who lived on the east shore of Lake Champlain. As it was mid-afternoon and none of us had eaten lunch, Dave and I climbed over a fence surrounding the marina on the mission of searching out a restaurant or store. Not finding any, we returned to our boats and took inventory on what food we had on board. Dave and

Margo produced hotdogs and had a portable grille to cook them on. Kathy and I produced some fruit and chips. Then we sat on board their boat and shared delightful conversation while we ate. When it came time to depart, we mutually agreed that we would continue our new found friendship.

Our totally unanticipated, unexpected meeting that day on another lake adventure led to a wonderful friendship which continues to this day. However, we no longer see each other as often as we did when we were lake dwellers. In retirement Dave and Margo moved to Arizona and we moved to Georgia. The day we sold 'Hav-n-Fun' was a sad day; however, our little boat had provided us many wonderful and happy memories.

The years we lived on beautiful Lake Champlain, were a wonderful time in our lives and reflection on lake adventures always inspires a smile.

6/04/04 – Last view of Hav-n-Fun Before Her Sale. She served us well.

SHORTS THAT FIT WELL

JUVENILE – RESTORATIVE JUSTICE

Upon reading the title of this story, most folks will assume a questioning look and say to themselves, "What is Juvenile-Restorative Justice?" That was my reaction when I read the employment want ad section of the Plattsburgh-Press Republican newspaper seeking Coordinator of a Juvenile-Restorative Justice program about to be implemented in Clinton County. The ad stated that Clinton County had received a federal grant for implementation of a Juvenile-Restorative Justice Program. The ad sounded intriguing and having recently retired from my second career, I decided to apply for the position. If I was hired, I would be performing work that I knew absolutely nothing about. I submitted my application, attaching a resume and personal credentials to the Commissioner of the Clinton County Department of Social Services, who would be overseeing and monitoring the program. I was surprised to receive an invitation for interview just two days after submitting my application. During the interview I learned that Restorative Justice was a program providing juveniles (in New York persons under the age of 16), an alternative to Family Court for resolution of their crimes. Juveniles arrested in Clinton County, for any and all crimes excepting Murder, would be provided the option of having their charge(s) resolved via participation in a "resolution conference;" which would involve the defendant, their parent(s), the victim(s) of their crime, a teacher or other representative from their school, the arresting police officer, and any other persons; such as a mental health professional, having an interest in the defendant juvenile.

The Commissioner advised that I would be provided a month to study and implement the program before receiving referrals. She also advised that I would be provided the assistance of two student interns, attending Master Degree programs in the State University of New York, at Plattsburgh. I would be required to train them concerning the restorative justice program and rate their performance as they would be receiving tuition assistance for participating in the program.

I was fortunate that two intelligent, ambitious college students; a male and a female, applied for the positions. Both were intrigued by the title of the program. Both quickly grasped the concept of restorative justice and applied themselves diligently.

As a retired police officer, I had arrested many juveniles during my career and was very familiar with the Family Court process. I frequently shook my head in frustration as probation was routinely assigned and then never truly enforced. The teen soon came to the realization that they could continue on the path to a criminal career without fear of punishment or reprisal. The term Restorative Justice triggered my curiosity and I became eager to learn about this new approach to dealing with juvenile crime. So I accepted the coordinator position and immediately commenced a cram course to learn as much as I could about the program.

Within three weeks, I submitted an outline to the Commissioner of Social Services, detailing how we would resolve the cases referred to us. It was quite an involved process, requiring lengthy interview of crime victim(s), a lengthy interview of the juvenile and his/her parent(s), and obtaining agreement from both parties that they would participate in a resolution process. Then a private setting was selected to conduct a restorative justice conference that would include victim, perpetrator, parent(s) a representative from the school attended by the juvenile and possibly a representative from mental health. Either myself, or one of my interns would moderate the get together and every attendee would be asked to openly participate. The desired goal was to have the juvenile accept responsibility for his or her criminal conduct, explain motivation for the conduct and accept the terms suggested by the attendees to restore justice. Our secondary goal was to assist the juvenile in resolving personal conflict. Our third objective was to provide the miscreant a new perspective on life so they would avoid future criminal conduct.

I decided to facilitate the first case referred to us and my interns would sit in as observers.

The first case referred, involved a 15-year old male, who had burglarized a neighbor's home and stolen a sum of money. The juvenile and his mother, readily agreed to bypass Family Court in favor of Restorative Justice. When I contacted the burglary victim his initial reaction was, "I am so angry with the (cuss words) kid that I want to rip his head off his shoulders! However, I am curious to learn why he stole from me, what he did with the money, and what he intends to do to regain my trust."

My first Restorative Justice conference actually went better than expected. Present at the session were: juvenile defendant, the victim, the defendant's mother, the arresting police officer, a school nurse and the Principal of the school attended by the defendant, who was interested in how our program would work. In turn, all were called upon to provide testimony and offer suggestions as to what course of action needed to be taken by the juvenile to resolve his criminal conduct. The juvenile testified that his parents had often argued and fought in his presence. He was very angry and confused when his father abandoned both he and his mother. After his father left home, his mother continually belabored him with complaints about his worthless father. He was confused and angry as to why his father had abandoned both he and his mother. The accumulation of frustration, anger, confusion and bitterness made him decide to leave home. However, he had no money and to get money, he broke into his neighbor's home and stole it. He intended to leave home the following day; however, the police arrived at his home the same day and busted him. (He was not aware that his crime had been witnessed by another neighbor in the trailer park development, who immediately contacted the police). He related that he actually liked the neighbor that he stole from and only took the money because he needed it to leave home.

The defendant's mother related the details of her broken marriage and admitted she had been sharing her frustration and anger with her son, not realizing the emotional toll it was taking on him.

The school nurse testified that the juvenile was emotionally troubled, was performing poorly in school and had been diagnosed as suffering from Attention Deficit Hyperactivity Disorder (ADHD), and was taking the prescribed medication Ritalin.

The victim of the crime related how angry he had been that his home was broken into and money stolen; however, after listening to testimony from the boy and other participants, he wanted a resolution that would set the boy on a straight and narrow path.

In conclusion, it was decided that, The Defendant juvenile would go to the victim's home once each week for two months and perform some sort of work, such as mowing lawn, or washing a car. The victim related that he would report to me the juvenile's compliance with the decision agreed upon. I was subsequently pleased to learn that the juvenile was complying and both victim and perpetrator had developed a warm personal relationship. After passage of nearly a year, I received a call from the victim, who related that the 'young man' whose head he had formerly wanted to rip off for stealing from him, had become like a son. He now took the boy fishing and they enjoyed each other's company.

I continued as Coordinator of the Restorative Justice Program for two years. During that time I facilitated numerous cases referred to our program. The crimes included: burglary, arson, larceny and criminal mischief. Some of the crimes were committed by male juveniles and some by female juveniles. Sad to say, not every one of those cases resulted in the success achieved in my first case.

I would point out, and it is interesting to note, that every defendant we dealt with came from either a single parent or broken home situation. All had emotional and anger issues and every one of them had been diagnosed as having Attention Deficit Disorder (ADD), or,

Attention Deficit Hyperactivity Disorder (ADHD), and all were taking medication to control anxiety and emotion.

As Coordinator of the program, I was required to attend a monthly Department of Social Security staff meeting, and summarize how the program was performing.

When my female intern graduated, obtaining her Master's degree, I decided to retire and recommended she replace me in the position of Coordinator. She was appointed and held the position until the federal grant funding the program expired and Clinton County decided not to continue funding. This fine young woman went on to obtain a career in the Department of Homeland Security and we remain friends to the time of this writing.

The two years I spent dealing with and resolving juvenile crime issues convinced me that the Restorative Justice Program was a valuable means of rehabilitating young people and motivating them to lead non-criminal productive lives.

Readers may be curious as to why I included this story in Shorts That Fit Well. I will explain that as I have not seen any news, or read any reports relating to restorative justice in several years, I wonder if the program is still in existence. As attorneys were generally not involved in the process and the majority of those in government positions of authority are attorneys, I doubt it. I believe the program achieved (limited) success and perhaps an interested reader will petition his or her representatives to reinstitute it.

SHORTS
THAT
FIT WELL

SMOKEY

While ensconced in my second career and living in Liberty, New York, one Saturday morning, I went to our local Agway store to purchase some sort of needed hardware item, and Kelly, our 8 year old daughter, accompanied me.

Upon entering Agway, I noticed a large steel wire cage near the entrance and the cage contained several kittens that were for sale. Kelly immediately focused on the kittens and she dropped to her knees in front of the cage to study the cute little 'fur balls. I told her to stay where she was and enjoy the kittens while I looked for the item I needed. When I approached the register at check out to pay for the item of hardware, Kelly grabbed my hand and begged me to purchase a totally grey kitten that had captured her heart. I winced and told her, "Honey, we already have a kitten, and they might not get along."

"But Daddy," she pleaded "this kitten is begging me to take him to our house."

I knelt down beside her in front of the cage and she pointed to an adorable completely grey kitten that was attacking the tails of its cage mates. When Kelly inserted her small hand into the cage, the grey kitten immediately came and rubbed its head against her fingers.

At the time, we owned a one-year old mischievous kitten, aptly named 'Mischief,' and I was not sure how Mischief would receive the company of another cat. However, as I gazed upon the happy scene of daughter and kitten, I thought, *oh well, both are female cats and I hate to disappoint my little girl.*

Kelly gave me a hug when I agreed to purchase the kitten and of course it was necessary to also purchase a catnip mouse, for our new baby's entertainment.

When we arrived home, Kathy eyed the kitten and asked, "Where did you find that little cutie? I thought you were going to the hardware store?"

Exhibiting a sheepish smile I responded, "Agway sells more than feed, hardware and tools. They also sell birds, kittens and animal toys. Kelly was smitten by the kitten and – look at her – how could I refuse?"

Upon entering our home, the kitten immediately checked out Mischief's food dish and located the litter box. Mischief studied the kitten, who immediately tried to engage her in play. The kitten's assault on Mischief's tail caused Kelly to squeal with delight. At first Mischief appeared to enjoy the play; however, as the play got rough, she stalked off, went to her cat bed, and the kitten decided to explore her wonderful new world.

While watching the kitten explore, we started discussion of selection of a name for our little grey fur ball. As the kitten was entirely grey we decided to name her Smokey.

On that day, at that time, I had no idea that Smokey would totally capture my heart and earn the 'one of my all time favorite pet awards.'

Smokey quickly asserted her authority over our home and knew how to tug at Kelly's and mom and dad's heart strings. It soon became apparent that Smokey was a very intelligent, very loving and very clean cat. She also quickly took charge of Mischief. Smokey would become disgusted when Mischief demonstrated sloppy eating, or sloppy litter box habits, chastising Mischief with a slap and growl. At feeding time, Smokey slowly ate her food and was careful not to slop any of it, whereas, Mischief gobbled her food and left a mess around her food dish.

While living in the Village of Liberty, we decided not to let Mischief or Smokey out of the house, for fear a dog would attack them, or they might get hit by a vehicle. When we moved to Lake Champlain, we started letting Smokey go outside during the day to hunt critters by the lake. She was very careful about staying at lakeside and did not venture out to the road in front of our home. Mischief seemed to have no desire to go outside.

Smokey proved quite a hunter and when she made a kill, she would bring it up onto our deck to proudly show us her prize. We knew when she had a trophy to show us because she would appear at the door and yowl. Kathy hated to hear that yowl, as quite often Smokey would appear with a small snake that she had killed.

My office in our Lake Champlain home, was on the second floor, and Smokey enjoyed lying on the sill of an open window, where she could watch me and keep track of what was going on outside. She spent so much of her time in my office that is where we placed her litter box. One weekend Kathy and I took a trip to visit Kathy's parents. As we would only be gone for two days, we decided that Smokey would be fine staying by herself. We put enough food out for her and she could use the litter box in my office. Knowing how much she enjoyed lying in the office window, I left it open, just enough for her to lie on the window sill. When we arrived home, Smokey greeted us at the door and meowed how happy she was to see us. Shortly after arriving home, I decided to go out on our deck to fill the two bird feeders attached to our deck railing. We kept a large bag of bird food in a very large wicker basket on our enclosed sun porch. When I went to get the bird seed, I discovered that Smokey had tipped the bag of bird food over emptying half of the bag in the wicker basket. Then she had used the basket as a litter box and covered up the evidence with bird seed. I was amazed that our always neat and clean kitty had used the basket as a litter box and equally amazed as to how she managed to tip over the 40 lb. bag of bird seed. Smokey sat watching me as I cleaned up the mess. I decided that she was angry with us for leaving her and took her anger out on us by using the bird seed as a litter box, and while cleaning up the mess, I scolded her, "You naughty kitty! I purposely filled your litter box with clean litter before we left and you did this! It is so out of character, shame on you!"

Smokey seemed to understand what I was saying and she led the way to the stairway leading to my office. As we started up the stairs I noticed that my office door was shut. After entering my office, I came to the realization that a gust of wind must have come in the open window and blew the door shut. Not being able to get to her litter box, our intelligent, always clean kitty knew the bird food was in the sun parlor and rather than mess on the floor, she made her own litter box. It was fortunate that Smokey was not in my office, when the door blew shut. When I realized what had happened, I picked Smokey up, held her on my lap, petted and praised her for her ingenuity.

In 2006, property taxes and cold winter weather were the motivating factors that caused us to sell our dream home on 'our lake.' We commenced looking for a comfortable home in the South. After looking at numerous homes in Tennessee, Alabama, North Carolina and Georgia, we purchased our present home, located only four miles from our daughter in Smyrna, Georgia. Smokey was now 15 years old and she did not want to leave her home on Lake Champlain. Furthermore, infrequent short trips to her veterinary were her only car experiences. She complained mightily during our two day drive to Georgia, even though she was allowed to be free in our car and Kathy held her on her lap during most of the trip. When we arrived at our Georgia home which was much larger than our Lake Champlain home, Smokey, explored her new digs and decided as long as she was with her 'peeps' the place was okay. There was a completely fenced in yard and she was able to hunt birds, chipmunks and other critters, though age was slowing her down. She spent most of her time looking for a lap to curl up on.

Sadly, the aging process began to take its toll on our dear, sweet grey kitty and she developed arthritis. Though hobbling about in obvious pain, she continued her cleanliness habits and her favorite time - I might add – mine too, was when we were in bed. She continued to place her head on my hand and purr contentedly, probably dreaming about her youth on the beautiful lake.

In cat years, Smokey lived to the old age of 17. Her arthritic pain became so severe that she limped slowly about and frequently cried out in pain. Her suffering brought us to tears and we made the decision to end her suffering. We took her to our Veterinarian, to be euthanized. It was a very sad time during which many tears were shed. We were able to find solace in realizing that Smokey had given us 17 years of love and affection. We are convinced that Smokey is now in Kitty Heaven and want her to know that she will always remain dear in our hearts and memory.

SHORTS THAT FIT WELL

TEENAGE REFLECTIONS

Recently, my wife and I were reflecting on events from our youth (something that old-timers occasionally do). It occurred to me that perhaps I should record some of our teenage experiences for our grandchildren as an analysis of what life was like in the "not so good" old days. There is a sharp contrast between teenage life then and teenage life now.

In 1950, a few months prior to my 12th birthday, Dad sold our three apartment home, located in Cortland, New York, and purchased a small (8-acre) farm located about one-mile south of the Hamlet of Sempronius, New York. Dad was convinced this change of environment – from city to rural – would not only reduce his property taxes but provide an escape from catering to the demands of lousy tenants and provide the means to produce most of our food. The move proved somewhat of a culture shock, as we had enjoyed conveniences in the city that were greatly lacking in the country. Our farm consisted of a white-wood clapboard house, good-sized barn, a chicken house and pig pen. Our move was in the spring season and we planted a garden immediately after moving in. The garden was large – about one acre in size. As we did not own a tractor, tiller and virtually no power tools, planting and caring for a garden with spades, hoes and rakes, required a lot of labor. Shortly after we settled in, Dad purchased a Guernsey dairy cow, a couple of steers (one Angus, one Hereford), four pigs and approximately 100 baby chicks.

Most of our little farm consisted of a grazing pasture, which had a trout stream that crossed through the middle. Eventually, Dad convinced his friend Walt Reynolds, who at the time was Sempronius Town Supervisor, to bring in a town owned bulldozer to create a pond in the pasture. In that bygone era, the Environmental Protection Agency (EPA) didn't exist and there were no required permits to fill out. The pond would serve as home to ducks, geese and for a time, a pair of Swans. It proved difficult keeping waterfowl, as Fox and Mink thought they were tasty morsels. Our cow provided all the milk we needed. We separated cream from the milk and churned our own butter.

In the fall of each year, we butchered a steer and a couple of pigs. At first we did not own a food freezer so Dad hung quarters of beef and hams from rafters on our back porch, which served as an open refrigeration area during the winter. Dad built removable wood panels to enclose the porch during the winter, to prevent critters from getting to our meat supply. Chicken was a frequent entrée in our home and my mother made the tastiest fried chicken in the entire area. I became proficient at lopping off a chicken's head and plucking feathers that gave way when immersed in boiling water.

When we moved into the farmhouse, the heating system was a combination wood/coal burning furnace located in the center of our cellar. Yes, we did have a cellar, which had a dirt floor and cobblestone wall foundation. One large cast iron register located in the center of our first floor, directly above the furnace, provided the source of heat for the entire house. We had appreciated oil heat in the city and this wood/coal monster was archaic in comparison. Of course, I soon learned how to stoke the furnace and when coal was burned (which was rare) how to properly vent the system to prevent carbon monoxide poisoning.

Mother and Dad's bedroom was located on the first floor, so during the winter they got to appreciate some warmth. The first year in the farm house, I shared a bedroom and double-bed with older brother Kenneth (Bud), and our devoted Beagle Sally. Our bedroom was located on the second floor at the windward side of the house. The only heat we appreciated was that which filtered up the stairway leading to the second floor. Some winter nights our exhaled breath produced an icy vapor. However, we slept comfortably hunkered under down quilts. Of course when crawling out of bed in the morning, we snatched our clothes and dashed downstairs to get dressed. When there was a snowstorm during the night, accompanied by wind, we would awaken in the morning to find snow had filtered into our room via gaps around the window casing.

When we moved into the farmhouse, we had running water; however, it would be more precisely correct to say 'trickling water,' as our water supply was a Spring located in the middle of our neighbor's cow pasture, about 300 yards up hill from our property. A shingled roof protected our water supply and prevented cows from wallowing in it. As the spring was on a hillside above our property, water easily flowed downhill, through a pipe leading to our house. We even appreciated a flush toilet and bathtub (no shower). However, upon flushing the toilet, refill of the tank would take 15-20 minutes. Bath water was via water heated on our kitchen wood stove, and our once a week bath was quite a process. During times of frost and freezing temperatures, the water was left running in our kitchen's large, cast iron sink, as continually flowing water (normally) does not freeze. I do recall a couple of cussing sessions when Dad had to use Kerosene to thaw out a frozen water pipe.

Brother Bud had graduated from Cortland High School, prior to our move to the farm. He sought employment with the Town Highway department and was hired. I believe that lasted only about one-year, as he enlisted in the U.S. Navy and served therein for the remainder of the Korean War.

One of Dad's greatest attributes was ambition. His idea of recreation, was traveling to the wood lot (about 10 acres) that he owned on Iowa Road in Sempronius, and cutting logs, fence posts and firewood, using a two-man crosscut saw, axes and wedges. Of course a two-man crosscut saw required someone on the other end and that man was either Bud or I. As an aside, I would point out that Claude Beyea was a virtual encyclopedia concerning trees and all of the various uses for wood. He could identify every type of tree, whether it was hard wood or soft wood and which wood was best suited for construction; which wood had the best burning and heat quality and virtually everything there was to know about forestry.

In the 1940's before moving to the farm, Dad, Bud, Uncle Fred Beyea and Wayne, built a good sized log cabin on the wood lot property, using only hand tools. Uncle Fred and 10-year old Wayne dug the modified cellar for the cabin's foundation with pick and shovel. It consumed nearly an entire summer. (This labor was also reported in He Was a Forty Niner).

After enduring a lack of amenities during our first year on the farm, Dad hired a well driller to drill a well, and we were suddenly blessed to have gushing water. That same year, he converted our center register only-furnace, into a wood/coal heating system with heat pipes and registers throughout the house. He took our kitchen wood stove to the log cabin and replaced it with a propane fueled gas stove. During either 1952 or 53, he purchased a chest type food freezer, and in 1953, he purchased our very first television set. As I recall, it was a floor console having about a 12 or 14 inch oval screen. We only received two or three channels (all programmed out of Syracuse, New York), in black and white and every channel's images were portrayed in a snow storm. The television stations went off the air at midnight and returned to the air around noon the following day. Shows that come to mind were Sid Caesar and Imogene Coca, Milton Berles Texaco Hour, The Ed Sullivan Show and (something) Theatre. Each day's programming ended at midnight and stations went off the air after the playing of our National Anthem. In the morning stations commenced programming by presenting Kate Smith, singing God Bless America.

We were blessed to have a telephone at the farm house. It was a pre-rotary 8 party line system. Each party on the line was assigned a specific number of rings. As I recall, ours was four. When placing a call you removed the phone from its cradle and if the phone was already in use, you either hung the phone back on its cradle, or eavesdropped on the other party's conversation. You can guess which option was normally taken. If the line was not being used, when you put the phone to your ear, a –live not recorded– operator, located in Moravia, New York, would say, "This is your operator. Number please." Operators were generally fountains of knowledge and were able to answer all sorts of questions. If you had an emergency and the line was busy, you informed the persons conversing that you needed to make an emergency call. Following correct protocol, they would hang up and of course after allowing a couple of minutes for the call to be placed, pick up again and listen in.

Upon our move to the farm that fall, I was enrolled in the 7th grade at Moravia Central Middle School. Hailing from the city, I was accustomed to walking to school and had never ridden a school bus. It pleases me to recall that all through elementary school, I was a straight A student. Transition to farm life would change my outlook on life and alter my scholarly achievements.

My very first day of riding the school bus, proved quite memorable. The bus stopped at the entrance to our driveway and I climbed aboard, a little timid, because I was the new kid from the city; as yet, did not have any friends and did not know how I would be received. I walked down the center aisle looking for a seat and recognized – although I did not know her name – a pretty neighbor girl sitting in a seat by herself. She invited me to share her seat. Immediately after sitting down, I felt a tap on my shoulder and turned around, to be stunned by a sucker punch delivered by an older boy. The totally unexpected blow stunned and surprised me more than hurt me and I stared at my assailant in shock and amazement. He threatened, "She's my girl, so don't get any ideas!" I was embarrassed, confused and did not respond. There was no need to respond because Mary Jane, my seat mate, who would subsequently become my girlfriend, glared at the fellow and said, "I'm not your girlfriend." At the same time, our bus driver, who had seen the action in his overhead mirror, yelled, "Hey! No fighting!" Fate plays a strange hand in later years my assailant on that first day of school, would marry my cousin.

One afternoon shortly after leaving school, our school bus driver was required to take a short detour across a narrow dirt road. Upon meeting a truck coming from the opposite direction, our driver drove to the right as far as possible to give way and the shoulder of the road collapsed. Our bus rolled off the road and came to rest on its right side.

All of the kids sitting on the left side of the bus were thrown out of their seats and the kids on the right side of the bus were at the bottom of the pile of kids. I was one of those on the bottom. However, the bus had been going very slow and as I recall, the only injuries suffered were bruises. As the bus door was on the right side of the bus, it could not be used and some kids were a little panicky. Our driver, assisted by some older boys managed to open the emergency door at the rear of the bus, jumped off the bus and then assisted all the kids off the bus. The roll over occurred only about two-tenths of a mile from school. Having no two-way radio or cell phone, our driver stayed with the bus and a couple of high school boys walked back to school and reported the roll over. Another bus was sent to pick us up and of course I was late arriving home that evening.

In that era, the bus rollover was just an exciting experience. No parents sued the school and there was no television or media coverage. A similar occurrence in today's litigious society would likely result in response by emergency personnel, television coverage, all kids taken to the hospital for examination and lawsuits against the school bus driver and the school.

Kathy would follow a similar path moving from the city to the country. In 1948, when she was 8 years old, her father moved his young family from Lansing Avenue in Cortland, New York, to a 96-acre, decrepit farm located outside the Village of Groton, New York. Her father's (Gregory), motivation for moving from the city to a farm, closely paralleled Claude Beyea's earlier stated motives.

Our children may recall, for we have told the story often, (story told in God Works in Mysterious Ways), as tykes, Kathy and I were neighbors in Cortland. We moved from that neighborhood around 1942-43 and I did not see Kathy again until I had been discharged from the military and she was in nurses training. We were paired on a blind date and I guess she was truly blind at the time, because she deserved better.

The farm that the Marion family purchased had more acreage that the Beyea farm; however, the old farm house had even fewer amenities. When they moved in, their bathroom was an outhouse. Water was provided via a hand pump located in the kitchen. Weekly baths were taken in a huge wash tub, and the house was heated by the same type coal/wood burning furnace having one center floor register. Like Claude Beyea, Gregory Marion was ambitious and worked very hard to not only provide for his family, but improve their living conditions. He gradually made renovations on the home, turning it into a comfortable environment. The Marion's were also on a multi-party phone line and their first television was purchased in the mid-fifties.

As earlier reported, my brother Bud joined the Navy in 1951 and his departure seemed to double my work load and worsen Dad's temper. To show respect for my parents who mellowed a great deal in their later years, I will not elaborate on the details of the cause of my leaving home.

In June, 1952, two months before my 14th birthday, I left home and became a hired man on a dairy farm owned by a young married couple. Their farm was located only about a mile from my parent's home and they were acquainted (as was everyone in a 10 mile radius of Sempronius) with my mother and father. My new boss and his wife, were in their 30s, and had two young children; a boy and a girl. The husband operated the dairy farm and his wife was a County Health Nurse. Her income greatly supplemented the meager income from her husband's dairy operation. Lawrence and Lola Heath were easy going and both exhibited happy dispositions. In his mid-30's Lawrence was blessed with thick dark hair and he was a very handsome man. He was muscular, had a trim build and two of his most desirable qualities were a warm personality and seemingly always present smile. Lola, also in her mid 30's, was of medium build and had premature salt and pepper hair. Lola seemed always upbeat and she was an excellent cook. Lola and Lawrence were a devoted couple with two children, Sharon, around 10 years old, and Roger, about 8 years old. Lola's ambition was amazing. She somehow, held down a full time job as County Health Nurse and took meticulous care of her husband, children and home. The couple warmly welcomed me into their home and introduced me to the farm operation. I would appreciate my own room while living with them in their large, early Colonial style, brick construction home, and shared all meals with the family. The ground rules were that I performed all assigned work to the best of my ability, treated the family with respect and kept my room neat. As the 'hired man' during the winter and school year, I was required to arise at 4:30 a.m. and proceed out to the barn. I fed all the animals then, assisted with milking. After completion of milking, the gutters also referred to as 'drops' had to be cleaned and disinfected. This required backing a manure spreader into the cement pathway that separated two rows of cows that were in stanchions. As Lawrence did not have an automatic gutter cleaner, we used square pointed shovels to clean the gutters and fill the spreader. During much of my first year on the farm, Joe and Ned, a team of huge but docile work horses were used to pull the spreader and our hay wagon. I never did quite get the hang of harnessing the horses, and Lawrence managed that. After completion of morning chores, I rushed into the house, took a quick shower, changed into school-clothes, snatched breakfast and managed to catch the school bus that stopped in front of the house. After arrival home from school in the afternoon, feeding animals and milking were repeated. We usually concluded the evening chores by 6 p.m. During the summer, having no school requirement, I had the luxury of starting the day at 5 a.m. The major difference between morning and evening chores was that after finishing milking in the morning, the 'drops' had to be cleaned. After completion of about six months on the farm, Lawrence purchased two John Deere tractors; a Model A and a Model B. We utilized the Model A for heavy tasks and the Model B for lighter tasks.

I cannot recall what Lawrence did with Joe and Ned. They were wonderful horses, but they were old and had served faithfully for a long time. Although I never became proficient at driving a horse team, I soon became proficient at operating a tractor and enjoyed that part of farming very much.

During my three plus years on the farm, in addition to my room and board, I received a salary of $10 per week in the winter and a whopping $25 per week in the summer. As I had virtually no time for frivolity, I saved my meager wages and was able to purchase my first car at age 15. It was a 1936 Plymouth coupe, color black. It had a standard transmission, floor mounted shift and you might get a kick out of learning the windshield defroster consisted of a small fan mounted on both sides of the windshield that was electrically operated. Having a car permitted me to get a later start for school in the morning and it provided transportation to take Mary Jane out for an occasional date.

Dating was very occasional as I was basically working every day from before dawn to dark.

While living and working on the farm, I had the luxury of having every other Sunday off. I would have a Sunday off and the following Sunday, was my boss's day off. Otherwise, every day began before dawn and usually ended at dark. I was pleased that during the spring of my senior year in high school, Lawrence told me I could stay after school to play baseball and I did. That would be the only sport I participated in throughout high school. I alternated between center field and right field. As I have always been a slow runner, I was much better at the plate with a bat in my hands than I was in the field.

I quickly learned that Lola was an excellent cook and I was a teenager with a prodigious appetite. I still recall many of the desserts that she prepared (they were scrumptious) and she encouraged me to eat all I wanted.

I attended Moravia Central School, located on Main Street in the small Village of Moravia, about ten miles distant from the farm. As previously stated, my work required my presence on the farm in the afternoon and therefore, I was not able to participate in after school activities, such as sports, theatre, clubs, etc.

Moravia High had a cafeteria and lunch program. I would point out that there was no government funded free lunch program in that era and students either paid for their lunch, or brought lunch to school with them. After my freshman year, I seldom ate in the cafeteria, opting to take my lunch break at "Ken's Snack Bar" a small luncheonette located next to the school grounds. The owner, Ken Reynolds, was one of eight Reynolds brothers, all residing in the area and all well known. You were already introduced to Walt Reynolds, who at the time was Sempronius Town Supervisor. At Ken's I could purchase a hot dog and drink for 25 cents and play a pin-ball machine while eating lunch. A game of pin-ball was 5 cents and if the player achieved a high enough score, free games were rewarded. I often had to return to school leaving free games on the machine.

In that era, political correctness was unheard of and there was little concern about damaging one's self-esteem or damaging a classmate's feelings. Everyone had to suck it up and fend for themselves. At Moravia

Central, the 'Townies' (kids who lived in, or, near the Village) had their own clique and the Townies would not associate with 'Smelly Farmers.' Townie boys were the school jocks and Townie girls (referred to as chicks), were members of the cheerleading squad and participated in school plays. As a 'Farmer' the only resentment I felt in that segregated atmosphere was being spurned by a couple of Townie girls that I was interested in dating. During my junior year, my resentment disappeared because Mary Jane (my first seatmate on the school bus), who was a freshman, became my steady girl friend.

I have already related the details of my first car purchase and having a car permitted me to visit Mary Jane and take her on dates. One of the places I took her during one of my Sunday's off was the Moravia Bowling Alley located at the intersection of Main and Cayuga Streets in the village. (The building was torn down in later years and replaced by a grocery store). The bowling alley, owned by Bob Becker, consisted of six lanes and snack bar. Bowling would become one of my favorite pastimes and in that era, I was quite proficient at scoring. During my junior or senior year of school, I paid the required entry fee to enter a men's league bowl off and won first prize with a combined three game total score of 668.

Like the Reynolds family, the Becker family consisted of many brothers, all living in the area and I knew most members of the family. Bob asked me if I would be interested in working as a pin-setter for men's league, which bowled on Friday evenings between 7-11 p.m. As I owned a car, I knew, by skipping supper at the farm, I could arrive at the bowling alley in time to grab a snack and work the alleys. Four hours of pin-setting paid $6. When I became proficient, I started working two alleys (referred to as jumping alleys) and earned $12. It was a dirty, dangerous job as the pit was small and the pin-setter had to be on constant alert to avoid being hit by flying bowling pins. During the almost two years that I worked the alley, I was never seriously injured, although I had a couple of close calls of being hit by careless bowlers who started throwing practice balls without checking to see it the pin-setter was in the pit. As there were just six alleys, the men's league had two shifts of bowlers. Thirty bowlers (6 teams consisting of 5 on each team) bowled between 7-9 p.m., and thirty bowled between 9-11 p.m.

I got to know many of the men and they would send cokes down to the pit as a tip. I soon became friends with Jimmy Dann, who usually worked with me during that time and we remained friends throughout life. Jimmy kicked around at various jobs after completion of school, and when a State Prison was constructed just outside the Village of Moravia, he obtained employment as a Correction Officer. I do not recall the names of the other kids who worked with me at the bowling alley, probably because most were not regulars.

As previously mentioned I bought my first car at age 15 and I was driving without a license or insurance. No adults ever expressed concern about my driving minus license and insurance. Upon turning 16, I sold my 1936 Plymouth and purchased a 1950 Dodge sedan, color white, having a standard transmission with 'fluid-matic' drive. Fluid-matic was sort of the forerunner to the automatic transmission. With fluid-matic you could stop at a light or intersection, leave the car in gear with your foot off the gas pedal and start out by pushing the gas pedal and not using the clutch. The problem was there was a one or two second delay from the time you depressed the gas pedal until the transmission dropped in gear, which resulted in a jerky start.

During that era most dairy farmers could not afford to purchase all of the machinery required for all of the various farming functions, so they formed a cooperative. What that means was: that each farmer purchased a different piece of farm equipment and then shared its use with other farmers. Farmers travelled from farm to farm to aid each other in baling hay, harvesting grain, cutting corn and silo filling, etc. I enjoyed travelling from farm to farm to perform the various tasks because I learned to operate all sorts of equipment. However, my fondest memories of those cooperative work details, was the feast that we always enjoyed, prepared by the wife of the farmer hosting the work detail. Delectable steak, roast beef, ham, turkey, or chicken were the entrees (and often there were more than one) accompanied by potatoes, vegetables, salads, Switchel, and concluded with pies, cakes and ice cream. The word 'switchel' will be foreign to most readers. Switchel was a very refreshing, thirst quenching drink made by the farm wives by combining lemon, vinegar, salt and sugar in a jug of water. It may not sound tasty, but when stirred, it was a delicious, thirst quenching drink.

It may seem strange, but during those teenage years (14-17), as a hired farm hand, I was treated as an adult. The only occasions I received an ass chewing (verbal only) came as the result of having damaged a piece of equipment, or operating equipment recklessly.

Of course I nurtured a desire to become acceptable to the money kids that comprised the 'Townies' and during my junior year, I discovered that they loved pranks and by performing pranks that got their attention, I began to endear myself with the 'Townie' boys. (Townie girls were never too keen on me). Although I was probably viewed as a Jester and a loser, they enjoyed my Jester antics. I am now embarrassed and ashamed to recollect some of my antics and mentally labored over whether to include any of them in this teenage chronicle. I will preface the telling of two of my pranks by acknowledging that what I did was unacceptable behavior in today's society. I can well imagine that one or more of my antics – if carried out in today's world – would result in possible arrest or classification of being A.D.D. or A.D.H.D and placement on probation and Ritalin. Having created and supervised Clinton County's Juvenile Restorative Justice Program in the mid 90's, I am a firm believer that today's sociologists, psychologists and child behavior experts are damaging our nation's young people through mislabeling of behavior and requiring the mandatory consumption of Ritalin, which is a powerful, mind altering, narcotic drug. I know, because virtually every kid in my program was on Ritalin and I observed how it was affecting them. I count my blessings and know I am fortunate to have lived my teenage years during an era when discipline, although sometimes harsh, was practical and did not impact the kid's future life. In today's society, my antics would have prevented me from joining the military. They certainly would have prevented me from being accepted into the State Police and I probably would have ended life stuck on a dairy farm. Having concluded a long dissertation concerning concepts in dealing with child behavior, I will report the details surrounding two of my antics.

First, I would point out that several incidents of note occurred during the couple of years I rode the school bus. There were fights on the bus that were always short in duration as they were quickly broken up by the driver. I had many different bus drivers and sometimes when our regular driver was absent, School Transportation Supervisor, Art S. drove our bus. Art was a no-nonsense disciplinarian. I recall that on two occasions during my ride home from school, Art stopped the bus and ordered miscreants off the bus. I recall one kid responding, "How am I supposed to get home?" As Art closed the bus door he yelled in response, "You should have thought about that before acting stupid!" Never knew how those kids got home but would guess they hitched a ride or walked, because there were no cell phones then.

During one blizzard type snow storm, school closed early due to the weather and busses arrived to take us home. On the way home, the bus I was riding on became stuck in a snow drift. As an older boy I helped the driver put tire chains on the wheels. We then managed to get free and arrived home safely.

Probably, the most memorable ride was the afternoon a Baptist Minister was our substitute driver. When some kids started acting up, he stopped alongside the highway and sermonized to us for about a half hour. A Catholic girl on the bus, informed her parents about his preaching and their complaint to the Superintendent of Schools ended the preacher's career as a school bus driver.

During my junior year, Mr. Jones, who wore the hats of: Vice-Principal, Basketball Coach, Social Studies Teacher, Guidance Counselor and Drivers Ed Instructor, purchased a bright red Volkswagen Bug, which he was very proud of. As Mr. Jones, was about 6'6" tall, it was quite comical to see him driving the Bug. One morning a group of 'Townie' classmates asked me (probably because of my size and farm hardened muscles) to help them pull off a prank. During the first class break, a group of us went outside, hefted the VW, carried it up two flights of concrete steps and placed in on the porch at the school's rear entrance. The school was soon abuzz and we began to worry what action would be taken. I would point out that in that era there were no police 'resource officers' in schools and the school principal was at liberty to mete out punishment he deemed appropriate. During the 2nd period, our school principal's voice suddenly boomed over the school intercom, "Mr. Jones car is presently located on the rear porch of the school. It will be returned to its place in the parking lot by the beginning of 3rd period. If it isn't, those students responsible will be suspended!" At next class break, we scurried outside and carried the VW back to its place in the parking lot.

Fast forward to today. The same prank would most likely result in a police response, an investigation would have been conducted and the students responsible arrested. They would be forced to appear in Family Court, be represented by an Attorney and eventually permitted to enter a plea bargain that involved placement on probation for a specific period of time. In that era, the incident was easily resolved. Mr. Jones had a wonderful sense of humor and he was provided a humorous story to share with his grandchildren.

During my senior year, I pulled a prank that if done today, would have resulted in arrest, probably prosecution, likely psychiatric evaluation and a declaration that I was in need of probation and counseling. In that era, it was merely a "double-dare" prank strongly motivated by an offer of $20 from Townie Boys, if I pulled it off. On the first day of our senior year, every boy in our class took a sudden liking to English. Our motivation was our new – fresh out of college – drop dead gorgeous English teacher. Practically every guy in my class dreamed as to how wonderful it would be to have Miss (I forget her name), as their girlfriend and realized that was not possible. About a month into the semester, 'Townie Boys' offered me a reward of $20 for kissing Miss?, in front of our entire class. I accepted the challenge without giving much thought as to how much trouble I would be in. Miss? (I can envision her pretty face, but cannot remember her name) was about ten minutes into teaching and standing at the front of the classroom. I arose from my desk and slowly walked to the front of the room. She stared at me displaying a look of curiosity as I approached her. Upon reaching her, I put my arms around her, bent her over and kissed her. When I released her, she slapped my face, then, ordered me to report to the Principal's office. After giving my class mates a high sign, I left the room and reported to Mr. Brooks, our school principal. Upon learning why I was there, Mr. Brooks, displayed a slight grin and asked, "You did what?" I explained about the challenge to kiss Miss?, and I did. While pondering what action to take it appeared to me that Mr. Brooks was imagining what it would be like to kiss Miss?. I was surprised and relieved when he told me to return to class and apologize to Miss? in front of the class and explain why I kissed her. I did as instructed. My apology was accepted and Miss? and I got along very well the rest of the year, which I ended with a grade of B.

One of the most memorable events from my teenage years on the farm was hurricane Hazel, which I believe hit the area in the summer of 1955. The day before Hazel struck my boss, Lawrence, drove one of our John Deere tractors, with Hay Baler attached to his parent's home in McGraw, New York, a distance of some 20-30 miles. I drove over later in his pickup truck which we used to return to Sempronius. After chores the next morning, we returned to McGraw in the truck. On arrival, we started baling hay. Lawrence drove tractor pulling the baler and I gathered bales of hay from the field, piled them on a wagon then, delivered them into the hay mow in his parent's barn.

Around noon, Lawrence's father appeared and informed us, "I just heard on the radio that a severe storm with damaging winds is expected to come through this area."

Around 3 that afternoon, the sky to our south turned ominously black and the look on Lawrence's face indicated he was concerned. He said, I want you to return to Sempronius and start milking a little early, in case the power goes off. You know if it does, we will have to milk by hand. I will finish baling this field and I will return home in my father's car."

When I departed from McGraw, it was very hot and the air was muggy. I arrived at our farm in Sempronius at around 4 in the afternoon. I was concerned because the sky was eerie looking and looked very menacing. Although the sun was shining brightly, the sky to the south was pitch-black. I brought the cows in from pasture, secured them in their stanchions and commenced milking. I do believe the Good Lord played a role in saving the barn from destruction, which could have very well resulted in my death or injury. Amazingly, a pregnant cow would be God's means of protection. At the time, one of our cows was very pregnant with calf and her date of delivery was near. As a result she was 'dry' and not being milked, so we left her in the barnyard while doing chores. Shortly after I started milking Hazel struck with fury. I lost electricity and started milking cows by hand. First our combination brick/wood chicken house located near the barn blew apart. I watched helplessly from a window in the milk house as chickens were scattered by the wind. While pouring a pail of milk into the strainer placed atop a stain-less steel milk can, lightning struck a lightning rod on top of the barn, then travelled down the ground wire, located between silo and milk house. I watched in horror as blue flame traveled from can to can, then across our milk cooler. Thank goodness the south side of the barn was located below ground. Knowing this gave me a sense of security; however, as I returned to the stanchion area from the milk house, I gulped in panic upon noticing the overhead door that provided entry and egress for the cows was bowed inward from the force of a howling wind. If that door had given way it was an almost certainty the barn would be torn asunder. Thank God for our pregnant cow, who probably weighed around 900-1000 pounds; she was standing in front of the door, head down, front legs splayed to brace herself and her huge body blocked the wind and saved the door from giving way. To exacerbate my concern, almost at the same time, our silo roof was blown off and the silo partially collapsed. Though extremely frightened, I tried to maintain my composure and continued milking. Lawrence arrived home about the time the eye of the hurricane passed. We continued milking and he told me that trees were down all over and he had to take a couple of detours to get home. After the eye of the hurricane passed, the wind struck again with renewed fury. We finished chores and surveyed damage. Lawrence told me we would look for chickens in the morning and we needed to seek cover. We departed the barn and headed for the house. The eye of the hurricane had passed and the storm now resumed in full fury. The wind was so strong, we had to double over and carefully lift one leg at a time so as not to be knocked over. An object sailed by my head as we inched our way toward the house.

Lawrence yelled, "Watch out! Those objects hurtling by our heads are bricks!" He apparently recognized they were bricks from the chicken house that was torn asunder.

The wind was so violent the approximate 100 yard walk from dairy barn to house, took us about 20 minutes. Bent over, we carefully shuffled along slowly lifting and placing one foot at a time, while avoiding missiles of debris flying through the air. We finally made it into the house and hunkered down in the cellar until the storm was over. Fortunately, the rugged old brick construction house escaped damage.

After finishing chores the next morning we started searching for chickens and surprisingly most had survived.

About six months before graduation, all seniors met with Guidance Counselor Mr. Jones, who reviewed each student's academic record and helped them in selecting a college and college major. I knew my grade point average hovered right around passing so I had no plan to attend college and no source of funding for college. I would point out that government backed tuition assistance loans were not available then. The only means of financial aid was a scholarship. Minus a scholarship the parents of the college bound student paid for their child's education.

Mr. Jones scrutinized my poor academic record, looked me in the eye and said, "Son, you are fortunate to be graduating. I would recommend that if you want to have any sort of successful future, you enlist in the military. It just so happens, at this time, the United States Navy is offering what is referred to as a 'Kiddy Cruise.' What that means is, you can enlist in the Navy now and be eligible for discharge the day before your 21st birthday. A specialty school is guaranteed as part of your enlistment. The only stipulation is, you must graduate from high school to be eligible."

Having no desire to be a farmer in adult life, I immediately filled out the paperwork for the Navy Kiddy Cruise program.

In my senior year, I was 6'3" tall and weighed about 195 lbs. I was the second largest member in my class and the second youngest member of the class. I would be three months shy of my 18th birthday on graduation day. Although having no idea what lay in store for me as a sailor, I knew that Brother Bud enjoyed his Navy hitch and joining the Navy gave me a sense of security in knowing I was embarking on the future with a plan that didn't include farming.

Prior to graduation, our senior class, consisting of 39 soon to be graduates, went on a 'senior class trip' to Washington, D.C. and New YorK City. The parents of pretty little blond cheerleader Phyllis Heigle, were our chaperones. Those poor folks! We traveled to Washington via a train that we boarded in Syracuse, New York. It was the first time I had ridden on a train. It was a tedious, long ride and we whiled away the hours singing songs like, "99 bottles of beer on the wall." Approximately 80 % of our group had a bottle of booze squirreled away in their luggage and we anticipated partying hearty when we checked into our hotel in Washington. Would point out that in that era, all the illicit drugs in common use today, were virtually unheard of. Booze was the fuze that got a lot of kids into trouble. Virtually every one of my classmates smoked cigarettes and oddly, I did not. I had tried a cigarette or two when I was in 8th or 9th grade and found no joy or pleasure in sucking in and blowing out smoke.

At the time of our Washington trip, I had been accepted by the 'Townies' and we all communicated just fine.

Our three days in Washington, D.C. were a blast and some kids were more blasted than others. All of the museums, especially the Smithsonian were interesting. The Lincoln and Washington memorials were awesome, and the Capitol and Treasury buildings impressive. My favorite was Arlington Cemetery and getting to see the changing of the guard. Of course while touring during the day, those of us who had partied the night before were nodding off and nursing headaches.

While in Washington D.C., we stayed in the Ambassador Hotel and one late afternoon as four of us wandered about the hotel, wondering where the action was, we discovered an unlocked door that opened into a suite. Wondering what the suite looked like, we opened the door and walked in. Oops! Three elderly looking men still partially dressed in Army uniforms, bearing General rank stars, were engaged in a tete-a-tete with three young women. One of the Generals yelled, "Get your asses out of here," and we did. We fled the room and hoped the Army officers did not call hotel security, apparently, they didn't, as no one came looking for us.

During the afternoon of our 2nd or 3rd day at the hotel, I wandered into the cocktail lounge and happened upon 4 kids about my own age, sitting at a table conversing. They eyed me up and down and one kid speaking in a very southern drawl asked me where I was from. I decided to have a little fun, so I drawled in response that 'ah' was from Mobile, Alabama. They invited me to join them and I learned they were from a school in South Carolina and like me, in Washington on a school trip. We hit it off and I was invited to join the fellows in one of their rooms to have a drink and play poker. As I enjoyed both, I agreed to join them. The room happened to be located only four doors away from a room occupied by three of my female classmates. I managed to carry on my southern drawl in a believable fashion and we were hitting it off quite well. I was also winning at poker, which we were playing for nickels. We were all downing shots of Gentlemen Jack while playing and my southern drawl kept improving with each drink. Everything was going swell until my new acquaintances related there were three gorgeous Yankee girls from New York, in room #--- just down the hall. One of the Carolina boys bragged as to what he intended to do to the Yankee girl that had blond hair and brown eyes, before they left Washington. I recognized that he was referring to my classmate Judy Wheat, whom I adored from afar, as she wouldn't have anything to do with me. The group of Carolina rebels were shocked and surprised when I suddenly stood up and responded – something to the effect minus my pretend southern drawl: "You blankety-blank a-holes better not go near her. I ain't from Alabama! I'm a Yankee from New York and she is my girl. Needless to say, they did not take kindly to having been suckered and subsequently threatened by a Yankee. I was pummeled by six Rebels and thrown out of the room. My shirt was torn, my nose was bleeding; however, intoxication numbed all pain. Having it in my mind that I needed to warn Judy, I stumbled down the hall and knocked on her door. One of her roommates opened the door and studied me curiously while asking, "What happened to you?" I staggered into the room and knocked over a floor lamp in the process. Feeling like a fool; which, at the moment I was, I proceeded to caution them about the rebel boys down the hall and warned them to be careful. As I spoke Judy moistened a wash cloth and applied it to my bloody nose. The girls thanked me for my concern and advised they would be watchful and careful. Then I left and went to my room. Her nursing my bloody nose was the closest I ever got to Judy.

After our 4th day in Washington, D.C., we boarded a train and travelled north to New York City, which was last stop on our itinerary. We stayed at the Hotel New Yorker in Manhattan. Having only two days in the city, we crowded in visits to the Metropolitan Museum, Empire State Building and the Statue of Liberty. My fondest memory of New York was our matinee visit to Radio City Music Hall, where we saw the movie 'Serenade' starring Mario Lanza, followed with a live performance by the Rockettes. The train ride home from NYC was very subdued as a very tired group of kids caught up on their sleep.

Graduation came two weeks after return from our senior class trip and I was two months shy of my 18th birthday. The day following graduation I reported for induction into the United States Navy. I was sworn in with a large group of young men, all from central New York, at a naval Reserve facility in Liverpool, New York; then we boarded a plane at the Syracuse airport and flew to Annapolis, Maryland. Our plane arrived during the late evening and we boarded a bus that delivered us to Bainbridge Naval Training Facility. At 17, almost 18, I was embarking on an uncertain future; however, it was a new adventure. The Navy turned out to be a wonderful adventure. During the next three plus years I discovered self-esteem and matured into adulthood. I also got to visit exotic places in the world where abject poverty and splendid wealth, by outward appearances seemingly coexisted in peace and harmony. The Navy proved to be a very enjoyable experience that opened the door to an entirely new vision of life. I give silent thanks to Mr. Jones for unlocking that door for me.

One of the adventures from my Navy career, "My Personal Experience With Jaws," is included in another chapter.

My intent in recording the events of my teenage life is to provide a comparison as to how life has changed in the past 60+ years, but my more important intention is to encourage young readers to always have confidence in themselves and their ability to succeed. It is reasonably certain there will be times in life when you face adversity. I encourage you to never give up on yourself and always strive to perform to the best of your ability. The road to success has many pitfalls and detours; however, via ambition, perseverance and determination you will reach the dreamed of destination.

SHORTS THAT FIT WELL

BE MY VALENTINE

During my State Police career, I received many certificates and awards associated with solving crime, providing public service and in association with public speaking engagements. Of course every award was greatly appreciated and they added enhancement to my resume for a second career. However, one totally unexpected award, that would do nothing to enhance my resume, stands head and shoulders above all the certificates, plaques, and letters of commendation received from supervisors and officials. It was an award that moved me to tears and continues to produce moisture in eyes dimmed by age.

I include the telling of the story as the final chapter in this book because the award had so much meaning to me and I wish to pay tribute to those who presented it to me all those years ago. This is the story.

In the 70's, I was an Investigator in the New York State Police, with assignment in Kingston, New York. Our office or barracks as it was called then was actually located in the small hamlet of Hurley, New York. I was conducting investigation into several break-ins of residences, and small business's generally involving the theft of money, jewelry, radios, and games. The modus operandi (MO) of the perpetrator(s) and nature of the property being stolen caused me to believe the break-ins were being committed by a lone, young male burglar. It appeared obvious that whoever was responsible was on the path to a life of crime and I needed to put an end to his travel on that highway leading to destruction. One of the crimes involved the forced entry of the Hurley Reformed Church and the theft of several items from the church's nursery school. The most valuable item stolen in the crime was a combination record/disk stereo player. This theft was minor in comparison to items stolen in other break-ins the burglar had committed. About a week after the church break-in, my investigation into the overnight burglary of a small convenience-store resulted in my developing a suspect. The suspect happened to be a 15-yer old juvenile, who lived in the area. I obtained a search warrant for the home of the young criminal. The boy's parents were quite surprised when I served the warrant on them and claimed they were unaware of their son's criminal conduct. My search of the home was quite productive. I recovered the property stolen from the store and the proceeds of many other burglaries, including the stereo and other property stolen from the Hurley Reformed church nursery school. As the burglar was a juvenile, he was petitioned to Ulster County Family Court, which by all appearance seemed to be an honor to him. The property that had been stolen was returned to the rightful owners. After being placed on probation, he continued his life of crime and I would get to deal with him again. After arresting him for a 2nd time, fate or God intervened. Justice finally won out for the residents of Ulster County, when the parents of the young apparent career criminal, moved to another state where their son would become other police agencies problem.

A few months passed and on Valentine's Day, I was seated in my office performing the laborious task of writing reports. My concentration was interrupted by the building's intercom. The Trooper on desk duty, announced, "Investigator Beyea, please report to the station lobby. You have visitors."

Visitors to our station normally spelled bad news. I pushed my case files aside, uttered a sigh and said to myself, "Here we go again, I will never get these reports written." Then I made my way to the station lobby. When I opened the interior door leading to the lobby, I was shocked and surprised. A group of beautiful little kids greeted me and they were holding a huge handmade, perfectly shaped heart, edge adorned in frilly white. The handsome tykes were accompanied by their nursery school teacher, a lovely young woman displaying a delightful smile. A reporter and photographer from the Kingston Daily Freeman Newspaper accompanied the group of little ones and their teacher.

Across the huge heart was penned, "To Our Friend Inspector Beyea From the Hurley Nursery School." Affixed on the center of the huge heart was a smaller heart mounted on a white paper plate. The small heart bore the meaningful words, "My Valentine."

Though happy, smiling and extremely pleased, my eyes filled with water and I had to gather my composure before pictures were taken. What a wonderful surprise from the hands and hearts of beautiful little tykes.

The photo that recorded that precious Valentine Day surprise would appear in our local newspaper, accompanied by a brief description of why the students at the Hurley Reformed Church Nursery School, created and presented the lovely Valentine Heart to State Police Investigator Wayne Beyea. The photo and its accompanying article appeared in the newspaper, and resulted in boosting my reputation in the community.

I treasure that Valentine's Day surprise more than all of the other awards received during my police career. Reflection on that happy moment inspires great joy and aids in keeping an old fellow young.

The End

Printed in the United States
By Bookmasters